Praise for *Opening to Divine Intervention*

"*Opening to Divine Intervention* may be the most important work of the 21st Century! Karoleen's book helped shift my God awareness and knowledge by considerably sharpening my ability to connect intuitively and spiritually. I was blown into a whole new dimension of understanding, comprehension, and existence."

> — Curt Swarm, Newspaper Columnist, Artist, and Author of *Task Force IED*

"Karoleen Fober's book, *Opening to Divine Intervention*, is THE GUIDE we need for these times of unprecedented change on our planet! It teaches us how to connect with our own intuition and Divine Guidance, which empowers us to become the best possible version of ourselves, enabling us to lead fulfilled and connected lives."

> — Cindy Anne Mathers, Certified Transformational Leader and Author of *DELVE-ing into Cultural Humility: How Respect and Deep Listening Can Heal a Nation*

"*Opening to Divine Intervention* is a beautiful book designed to awaken the spiritual communication and connection with our divine team. And you will love her ACUTE System! It's an accurate tool that instructs you how to connect spiritually."

> — Laurie Hazel, Author of *Love Letters From the Angels*

"No matter where you are on your faith journey, *Opening to Divine Intervention* will help you build your spiritual framework. Karoleen's stories offer a way to see life with more awareness, beauty, and a wider lens. I'm left with a renewed sense of energy for people, connecting, trusting my intuitive instincts, and manifesting my dreams. This book will transform your life!"

> — Kate Wirtjes, BSE Chemical Engineering,
> MS Engineering Management, Environmental Engineering
> Manager, John Deere

"*Opening to Divine Intervention* will change your life—and change it for the better! Finally, a book chock-full of real-life stories and much needed clarity for your ability to connect to the Spirit of God—which every single person possesses. Karoleen will help you discover a new awareness of your intuition, how to confidently trust it, and how it has been there and served you in amazing ways throughout your life. This book is an invaluable resource. Keep it close by."

> — Chequita McCullough, Minister, Transformational Coach,
> Author of forthcoming *Calling All Daughters: A Biblical
> Blueprint to Restore your Mother-Daughter Relationship*

"I laughed. I cried. Reading *Opening to Divine Intervention* felt like being wrapped in a cozy blanket by the fireplace, enjoying hot cocoa with your best friend. With each deeply personal story, Karoleen exquisitely shares how the many blessings of Divine Intervention are available to us all when we become more open and aware. If you desire to expand your intuitive abilities and grow spiritually, this is the book for you!"

— Anela Arcari, Intuitive Coach, NCC, Retired U.S. Army Officer, Executive Film Producer of *There's Got to Be More to Life,* Author of forthcoming *Becoming All You Can Be*

"Karoleen Fober has created a bridge for spiritual expression and communication, reconnecting today's believers to the metaphysical, the mystical, and the mystery. *Opening to Divine Intervention* encourages readers to step out of self-imposed limitations while giving everyone permission to be in conversation with God. Through reflecting upon her own spiritual journey and sharing stories of Divine communication, intervention, and blessings in the lives of others, Fober invites us to imagine what's possible with an increased awareness of Divine connection. She not only inspires, but empowers and educates with her ACUTE System for Spiritual Communication and 15 Types of Divine Intervention. Fober's courage and willingness to be transparent calls us to step into our fullest, most authentic, soul-aligned spiritual selves. Fasten your seatbelt—you will be forever changed by meeting Karoleen Fober on the pages of *Opening to Divine Intervention.*"

— Erin Moroney LaBelle, Psychospiritual Life Coach, Photographer, Writer

OPENING *to* DIVINE INTERVENTION

Expand and Strengthen Your Intuitive
Abilities and Spiritual Connection

KAROLEEN FOBER

Capucia LLC
211 Pauline Drive #513
York, PA 17402
www.capuciapublishing.com
Send questions to: support@capuciapublishing.com

Paperback ISBN: 978-1-954920-78-1
eBook ISBN: 978-1-954920-77-4
Library of Congress Control Number: 2023914711

Cover Design: Ranilo Cabo
Layout: Ranilo Cabo
Editor and Proofreader: Susan Bruck
Author Photo: Bo Studio 101 www.BoStudio101.com
Book Midwife: Karen Everitt

Printed in the United States of America

Capucia LLC is proud to be a part of the Tree Neutral® program. Tree Neutral offsets the number of trees consumed in the production and printing of this book by taking proactive steps such as planting trees in direct proportion to the number of trees used to print books. To learn more about Tree Neutral, please visit treeneutral.com.

I dedicate this book to my mom, Ethel May Morrow Harryman,
who modeled her beautiful life on the Golden Rule.

And to Gary and our family, my favorite Divine Intervention blessings.

To all the LightWorkers, for honoring your Divine gifts for the
Highest Benefit of All.

And to our Creator / God, for making everything possible.

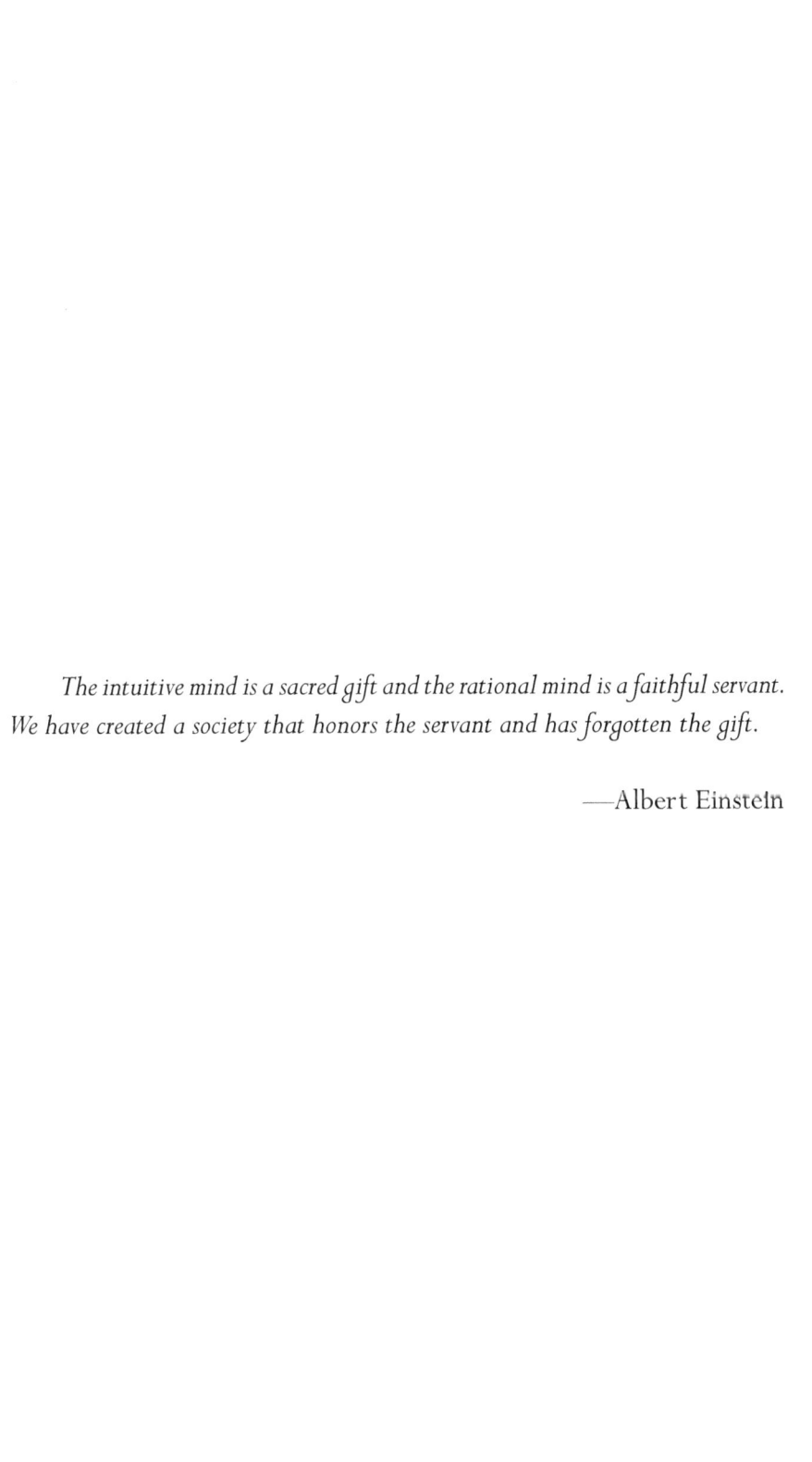

*The intuitive mind is a sacred gift and the rational mind is a faithful servant.
We have created a society that honors the servant and has forgotten the gift.*

—Albert Einstein

Contents

The Seed is Planted

It was 10:00 on a Saturday morning on January 15, 2000. There was excitement in the air. I was sitting on a metal folding chair in a big circle along with about thirty other women. I had signed up to attend a class on intuition and reading Divine Energy with Janine Ambrose, Ph.D. After the education part of the event, Janine, the Divine Energy reader, stood in front of each person and shared the Divine messages she received for each of us. About ten people received their readings before me.

I paid close attention to each person and what Janine said to them. Many of the women nodded their heads and smiled as they looked up at her, as if in agreement, like they understood what she was saying, and it was making sense to them. I was thoroughly enjoying myself and couldn't wait for my turn.

Throughout the time that Janine had been reading, I heard soft chatter and sometimes laughter among the other women sitting in the circle as they listened and waited for their turns. It wasn't distracting. It felt normal; people were responding to Janine's Divine gift.

So, when Janine stood in front of me with her eyes closed, holding her hands out in front of her with her palms facing up, I was ready! I'd brought along my notepad and pen. My pen was upright, standing at attention, poised to write down every word she said.

Suddenly, there was silence. The room had gone stone cold quiet. Everyone stopped talking. It felt as though everyone, including me, had also stopped breathing. I wrote down the first two sentences she said. And then I felt as if I had become paralyzed. My brain frantically tried to help me make sense of her words. And those words were, "You are going to write a book. And this book will be important for the world."

My Divine Intervention experiences, like the one above, sometimes scared or shocked me initially, especially when the experience or information was so unexpected. I was really startled by this information, and I don't remember anything else said to me or others the rest of that day. It affected me so much that I was disappointed with myself when I later realized that I didn't even think to ask her what the book might be about.

Seven years later, because I was so perplexed by this message, I hired Janine for a private reading. I hoped that she would be able to reconnect and give me more information about this book I was going to be writing. I wondered if she would remember or see what it might be about. Disappointingly, she had no new information about it and explained to me that she never remembers her readings. I carried on with life and put the idea of writing a book on the back burner.

Still, I energetically resonated with the words she had spoken to me that day, and I never forgot them. I kept wondering what in the world would this book—that I supposedly was going to write—be about? I hadn't a clue.

Through the years, I had two more predictions by two different Divine Energy readers that specifically talked about me writing "this book." Little did I know at the time of the first book prediction what wonders were to come into my life—how my life would be filled with so many and such widely varying Divine Intervention experiences. How the book that had been predicted twenty-three years ago would, in fact, be about the rich spiritual journey of my Divine Intervention experiences, including my very first Divine Energy reading where Janine predicted I would write this book! It feels right and fitting that the first Divine Intervention story I share with you is the one that has filled me with so much wonder and so many questions.

Introduction

My name is Karoleen Fober. I am a wife to Gary and a bonus mom and grandma. I grew up on a farm in Iowa and graduated with a B.S. degree in early childhood education from Iowa State University in 1979. I taught preschool handicapped children for four years and owned my own financial advising practice for fifteen. I sold this practice and created All Inspired Coaching and Consulting in 2001, and I am currently in my twenty-second year as an intuitive business and life mastery coach, with clients throughout the United States.

Yet maybe the most important thing to say about myself is that I am a child of God. This is how I think of myself first and foremost. Our Creator, who I refer to as God, is the Divine Entity who has given us a temporary home here on earth. We are part of a vibrant and vibrational Divine Energy System that continues to amaze, astonish, and still perplex even the most notable historians, scientists, and theologians. While I am not a historian, scientist, or theologian, I am someone who takes note of what is going on in this world of Divine Energy and of the continually evolving discoveries that have been documented about it.

But what has most captured my attention and captivated my heart and soul is my relationship with my Creator/God and this Divine Energy System that we have been gifted to live in. And not just since I had that mini-individual Divine Energy reading from Janine over twenty-three years ago. I've been captivated by my spiritual relationship with God since as far back as I can remember.

I consider myself to be a normal person, and I have loved all the joyful activities and relationships in my life that I've just mentioned. Yet, there were events in my life that I put in a different category entirely.

Throughout my life I have experienced moments and events that I kept to myself. These experiences held a different feeling and significance that I rarely talked about in my early years. They were hard to explain, hard to believe—and hard to deny. Many were supernatural, pivotal to my life, always helpful—in the long run—and always felt powerful. Undeniably powerful.

In my late twenties or early thirties, I found myself referring to these amazing and continually occurring "happenings" as Divine Interventions.

These experiences took my breath away. I felt they were directly linked to a loving and immensely powerful entity; I believed they came from God. I still do.

But life kept whizzing by. In my late twenties, when I became a financial advisor, I was so busy building my business and working that when a Divine Intervention experience happened, I only had a few seconds to take note and marvel about it before I moved on to the next commitment or demand.

And life didn't slow down when I married Gary when I was thirty-seven. In fact, it revved up, and ten months later, I became an over-the-moon grandma. Home and career moves, three years of coaching classes, building another business, and seven more grandchildren later, lots of wonderful living had happened. And lots of Divine Intervention had happened, too.

What to do with all this Divine Intervention? I thought of it here and there and smiled in silent knowing. I thanked God for it and pondered about these miracles in my life. Then I'd tuck them back deep into my heart and cherish them. And I moved on.

Finally, at the end of 2017, I stopped allowing myself to move on from all the Divine Intervention that I had experienced. It was time to sort it all out. Besides, I had grown frustrated with not knowing what subject I would someday write my book about. (Remember, God doesn't always reveal all the details of His messages on your time frame. He reveals them at the best time for your spiritual growth and lessons.) While I was still drawing a blank on my book's subject, I could at least make myself useful and get my Divine Intervention experiences written down.

If you had asked me how many Divine Intervention experiences I'd had at the time, I would probably have said there were maybe twenty. In my first attempt at listing them, I had thirty. Over the next two weeks, thirty turned into fifty.

With our winter getaway to Florida coming up, I focused on pinpointing the dates each had happened and putting them into chronological order. I had my precious list of fifty Divine Intervention experiences in my carry-on.

Once I was in Florida, as I looked at the list, I remembered every vivid detail as if it was happening again. Only this time, instead of individual events that had happened separately throughout my life, they were joined by a strong, yet invisible, powerful line of connecting energy that was alive and pulsating. What a feeling. My entire body tingled. I remember sitting there at my desk when a swirl of energy completely engulfed my being. Out loud, I said to myself, "Oh my God! THIS IS THE BOOK!!!!!"

Over the next five years, I added over two hundred more (and counting!) Divine Intervention experiences to my growing list and categorized them into fifteen types.

While all of them seem like Divine miracles to me, I refer to only a few as miracles. Some of the other fifteen categories are: Divine Energetic Readings and predictions; Divine pivotal moments in my life; Divine lessons; dreams and premonitions; human and heavenly Angels;

a near-death experience; natural healing and energetic alignments; prayers asked and answered and manifesting stories; and messages from deceased loved ones. I came up with my fifteenth category, which I call Natural Divine Phenomena, to include those experiences that dealt with nature and my environment. (I have included a list of these fifteen Types of Divine Intervention, with definitions, in Appendix 1.)

I also share the lessons that I learned from all my Divine Intervention experiences along the way, because God helped me realize they were universal lessons for all of us and wanted me to share them with others.

The book begins in 2011, right before I experienced the most pivotal and life-changing time of my life. The kind of experiences that change you forever—where you can't go back to being the person you used to be. I came face to face with undeniable spiritual points of no return. If one survives these, surrendering to the depths of despair has been known to lift a person to a heightened spiritual awareness, spiritual growth, spiritual acceptance, and unimaginable clarity. After healing from the anguish and pain of my mother's death, I found I had a new spiritual gift of mediumship. At that point I began to revisit and connect the Divine Intervention dots of my life, discovering and claiming an elevated spiritual awareness that has been part of my life since I was born.

While I came to understand that I have been highly intuitive my whole life and "known things" that I had no way of knowing how I knew them, I never really thought that much about it, and thought that everyone *knew things* like I did. I grew up in the 1960s and 70s, when the word *intuition* wasn't really part of my everyday language. It was much later when I began to be interested in opening to and deepening my spiritual connection, having a more direct partnership with my Creator/God, and began meeting other people who were also consciously on their spiritual path and intuitively gifted, as well.

Through the years, I have pieced together an explanation of my spiritual gifts by reading the Bible and many books by authors who have walked this path ahead of me. I have come to accept that we all have God's brilliantly designed and created intuitive abilities, but not everyone makes it a priority to recognize and use them.

I learned that most people stop utilizing their intuitive abilities somewhere between the ages of six and eight. It is quite common for younger children to communicate with God, Angels, and deceased loved ones on a regular basis. I've talked to many parents and grandparents who attest to this.

While our current culture doesn't always recognize, support, or teach about these God-given abilities, it is slowly moving in the direction of acknowledgment. Science understands that our souls are made up of electromagnetic energy that never dies but only transforms. I recommend Mark Anthony's book, *The Afterlife Frequency* (2021). He does a great job of enlightening us with his collection and explanation of scientific and historically-referenced documentation of how we can communicate with the Spiritual Realm.

We are fully able to communicate with this realm because our Creator designed us this way. Our Creator designed every system in our bodies, such as our respiratory system, our digestive system, and our electromagnetic heart and brain systems. And we have been Divinely designed to receive messages through His electromagnetic Spiritual Communication System.

And what about praying? This is the most basic category of Divine Intervention, one that most of us were taught as children. The act of praying signifies that we can connect with God, that God can hear what we are thinking and saying. This is Spiritual Communication at its core.

If you pray, it makes sense that you would be open to receiving God's answers. Praying is a psychic action. According to Google, the word *psyche* means "of the human soul, mind, or spirit." When you take a psychic action, you are interacting from your soul/mind/spirit. When you pray, you are communicating with God through your Divinely given vibrational soul—your electromagnetic soul—that God brilliantly designed for us to use.

Yet we often ignore all the Divine messages—our *answers*, *inklings*, and *feelings* that everyone is naturally set up to receive at birth. They are discounted, made fun of, kept hidden, or forgotten.

I believe this is because we fear being persecuted. Those who have focused on power, jealousy, and controlling others have persecuted those who received Divine messages throughout the ages. Jesus himself was persecuted for His Divine abilities and the miracles that he performed. He clearly stated that others could do what he was able to do—and even more than he did—in John 14. In both the Old and New Testaments of the Bible, people communicated with God and the Angels through the Spiritual Realm.

These stories of Miracles and Divine Intervention are a resource to help us maintain our lifeline to God and our spiritual home. When we read and learn about them, they nourish our souls and provide us with the reminder of how much we are loved, protected, and spiritually guided.

And I feel that God and His Spiritual Realm are still performing miracles and providing Divine Interventions for us all, here on earth, every day. But are we spiritually awake and aware enough to notice? Are we noticing all our Divine messages and miracles?

Many of us use Spiritual Communication every day, but we don't acknowledge it. Our gut feelings about people and situations turn out to be true. We are visited by our deceased loved ones in our dreams. We are given insight about a future event. Divine Communication is one of our greatest gifts for navigating life, yet do we appreciate it? So few of us give thanks for it. We rarely even acknowledge it.

Intuition is like an internal GPS and a Google-like Divine Energy resonating system combined, a Divine gift given to us at birth by our Creator. A gift that works for us all day, every day. When we acknowledge our intuition and use it through the years and learn from great teachers along the way, we can increase our abilities and accuracy, achieving higher levels of mastery to assist ourselves and others in navigating life here on earth. In 1 Corinthians 12:31, we are encouraged to strive for these greater Spiritual gifts, if that is our desire.

Intuition is our spiritual language, our language of origin, as souls in the Spiritual Realm. This Spiritual Realm, which I also call Heaven or the Other Side, is where God, all the Angels and spiritual guides, and our deceased loved ones are. We are all spiritual beings first and foremost. And while on earth, we are spiritual beings in a human body.

As a medium, I deliver messages from loved ones who have died and who step forward to offer beautiful messages of love, comfort, and guidance to remind us that their souls are still alive and watching over us. When I feel the messages of love and assistance that come through for their loved ones, it is always a most wonderful experience of connection for me. I never know who or what is going to come through, but it is always an amazing, beautiful, and touching event. I share each time that what will come through will be the most important messages that someone needs to hear in that moment and for the *Highest Benefit of All*. You may not hear what you want, but you will hear what you need most.

They say that love is the most powerful yet underutilized energy in the world. There are those who scoff at the abilities of intuitives and mediums. I admit that I might have been one of those skeptics, except for my undeniable experiences, many of which I share in this book. I feel privileged to serve God and humanity and witness the exchanges of love in these most powerful ways. Opening to and understanding that the love bonds that are created in our lives continue and never die is a blessing for me. I believe it can be a blessing for us all. It is with that intention that this book begins.

And I believe this is the book that Janine Divinely predicted I would write over twenty-three years ago. Whether it is an important book for the world remains to be seen. What I care about most, and hope for, is that this will be an important book for you.

Part I

A Change is Coming

CHAPTER 1

There is More for You

Everything was changing.
I could feel it, even though I didn't understand what was happening. Something strong had taken hold of me and wasn't letting go. It unnerved me, but I shook it off as best I could.

I'd just arrived back home to Iowa, in March of 2011, after our winter in Florida, where we'd gone to escape the ice, snow, and frigid temperatures. Florida was my husband's health plan after his surgeon told us seven years earlier that Gary could never fall again unless he wanted to spend the rest of his life in a wheelchair. Since then, as of 2022, he's had ten joint replacement surgeries on his hips, knees, and shoulders. I call him my "Bionic Man," and I'm happy to say he's not in a wheelchair and golfs three to four days a week. (More about Gary and his healing to come.)

I was fifty-three years old and had been working on a new creation for my business clients. I was paying another coach handsomely to help me launch a product online that would go nationwide. It was the biggest product I'd taken on thus far in my career as a business and life mastery coach. I'd spent a year delivering the content to a small group of clients and was getting ready to deliver it online to the masses. I felt the pressure to be productive, focused, and to Get It Done!

I had been making great progress and couldn't figure out why now, every time I sat down in my home office, I felt all my energy drain out of me. I went in feeling like a full glass of water, but every time I sat down to work on this project, the water leaked out. With a lack of focus, I'd stare at the computer, trying to will myself to concentrate, and rack my brain as to what was going on with me. It got so bad that whenever I walked into my office, I immediately turned around and walked back out.

The days and weeks went by. I emailed my coach several times to cancel and reschedule our appointments. I felt terrible but didn't know what else to do.

One day, I was so frustrated, I simply said, "God, please help me! What is going on here?"

And that's when I heard it.

The Voice.

I'd heard this Voice at different times throughout my life. I was still trying to figure out who the Voice belonged to, where it came from; I wanted to give it some kind of definition. But life went at a fast clip, and I'd get distracted back into my busy life full of family and work commitments, letting my questions dangle.

I knew this much: the Voice felt powerful. Sometimes, it was loud and almost commanding. Sometimes it whispered. Even without feeling confident about its source, it always got my attention, and it always stopped me in my tracks. It had happened enough in my life that I no longer felt afraid of it. I had an uncanny respect and trust in it without really knowing what it was. It felt protective and wise, as if it was always watching over me, and I admit I came to welcome it.

And one other thing. I always listen to it. I heed it, no matter what. The Voice said, "*More!*"

I said, "More? More what?"

The Voice said, "*There is more for you, Karoleen. More for you than this.*"

What I wasn't completely sure of then, but figured out later, was that the Voice was the Holy Spirit speaking to me. While this message was mysterious, I felt that it helped me see that what I was trying so hard to do was not on my soul's path. The lesson I felt I was getting at the time was that the project I was working on was a fine project to do. There was nothing wrong with it. It just wasn't part of my soul's mission. Every time I went into my office, I can admit now, my heart wasn't really in it. My energy draining was also my own inner wisdom revolting against something I was forcing myself to do.

I can see now that that project was something I felt I "should" do. It was a logical next step, a good project, but one that would take tremendous changes, effort, and time. I would have placed myself into a position with more responsibility, needed to hire additional staff, and, most importantly, do something I really didn't love.

I am so grateful for the Divine Intervention that happened that day. I've learned when I'm so frustrated and feel like I'm pushing myself up a hill, that's the time to take a Spiritual time-out and ask God for help.

God speaks through the Spirit (Holy Spirit) to us in times of dire need. Sometimes we are our own worst enemies. We become bound and determined to do what we think we should be doing. God and everyone in the Spiritual Realm know when we're off track. Because of the additional gift of Free Will, they do not attempt to micromanage us, but they will try to get our attention and help us get back on track on our soul's path. The question to ask is, will we listen to these important and helpful messages of Divine Intervention?

I could have chosen to try and force myself to continue with this project, but my body was not cooperating, and it would have been a disastrous decision, especially for what I would be facing in the months ahead, although I didn't know that part yet.

Years later, I labeled this a Divine Message, a Divine Lesson, and a Divine Pivotal Moment. I've found many Divine Intervention experiences can fit in one or more categories. By feeling the lack of energy, I thought God, or my Guardian Angel or something quite powerful, was once again guiding me towards something more, something better, something for the Highest Benefit of All.

Have there been times in your life when you have felt or heard that powerful Voice and/or a powerful energy pull?

What did you do?

How did you handle it?

What happened?

What was the result of your Divine Message/Divine Pivotal Moment?

CHAPTER 2

Mom in the Hospital

Because I had found myself physically and energetically unable to finish my big project, I finally called my coach and leveled with her. I shared the crazy energy drains and the message that there was something "*more*" for me even though I had no clue what the "*more*" was. Most coaches I have met and worked with are highly intuitive, so she got it and understood that I was tabling the project for now and maybe forever, which was probably more likely.

By this time, it was May, flower planting time in Iowa. I refocused my efforts on my pots and gardens of double hibiscus, dahlias, petunias, geraniums, impatiens, snapdragons, and pansies. I loved getting into the groove of being back in Iowa again, close to our family, friends, neighbors, and eight grandchildren. While Gary and I have fallen in love with our always magical and rejuvenating winter getaways to Florida, there's nothing like coming home.

The summer days of leisure were filled. Mornings were dedicated to the deadheading, weeding, watering, and overall tending of our flowerpots and gardens and catching up with the neighbors as they walked by or waved from their porches. Afternoons were for client calls, watching the grandkids splash around and score dives off the board at our neighborhood pool, or deck lounging with a good book surrounded by hues of vibrant tangerine, pink, yellow, purple, and blue. Evenings brought grilling and more deck time, watching the Cedar River laze by.

Life was easy and perfect.

Or so I thought. I would soon begin to understand what "*more*" meant.

My mom was a healthy, independent, and happy eighty-six-year-old. She lived in her own home, still drove everywhere, gave piano lessons three afternoons a week, played the piano and organ for church, weddings, funerals, and at the local hospital and nursing home. If she was asked to play, she did. She had excelled in music as a child and was given piano lessons from a young age, and she spent hours practicing daily and sharing her gifts. By the time she was in high school, Mom was musically in demand and loved it. And she sang. She sang mostly in the church choir, but she also sang while she played the piano if the moment allowed. She believed that God had blessed her with these talents and opportunities, and she made the most of them.

She grew up, graduated from AIB, the American Institute of Business, in Des Moines, married, reared her family, worked at the Cantril State Savings Bank for 30 years, retired, and volunteered, all in Iowa. She was tireless, a people person and a connecter. She knew everyone, and everyone knew her.

Her eighty-seventh birthday was coming up on September 18th. Gary and I planned to make the 3-hour drive down to Keosauqua, take her out to lunch and spend the day visiting with her, and drive back home to Cedar Falls all in one day. I'd talked with her midweek and told her I would call her when we were about thirty minutes away, like I usually did. So everything was set for that Friday.

Gary and I got on our way at about eight o'clock and expected to be at her house around 11 a.m. About ten-thirty, I called her on my cell phone, and there was no answer. I just figured she had gone down to the grocery store for something and thought nothing of it. I called her again about fifteen minutes before we arrived and still no answer. Hmmm. She's probably outside talking with one of the neighbors, waiting for us to roll in. Five minutes before we arrived, I called again. No answer. Weird.

Still not too concerned, I saw my brother, Lawrence's, car parked on the side of the house as we pulled into the driveway. I knocked on the door, but no answer. Mom normally left the door unlocked, so I opened the door, hollering as I entered, "It's me, Mom! We're here!" It was quiet.

Suddenly, I heard someone in the living room, and my brother walked into the kitchen from there.

"Hi! Where's Mom?" I asked.

His eyes got big, and his face looked shocked. He said, "Oh, no! Did I not call you last night?"

"Call me about what? No, you didn't call me last night!" I exclaimed with confusion. "What's going on? Where's Mom?"

He apologized and explained that he had been so exhausted from all that happened the night before with Mom, finishing his farming chores, and trying to get all the family called, he'd missed calling me.

"Mom's in the hospital. She went there last night."

He explained that Mom had gone somewhere with a friend the day before. After she got home, she wasn't feeling good, so she had her friend take her to the hospital.

I looked around. I saw trouble in the kitchen. Mom's medications were scattered all over the kitchen table. There was a banana laying on its side, peeled and uneaten. Mom was a social butterfly. She was always rushing around trying to do all the many things she wanted to do. My panic button arm-wrestled me for control. Had she forgotten to take her medicine, dropped the bottle, and then not felt good, and called her friend back? My heart sank, and my brain was on high alert.

"Well, let's get out to the hospital now, and you can fill me in on everything once we are there. I want to see and talk to Mom," I said, trying not to panic.

Breathe, Karoleen, breathe. Save your energy for Mom.

So we got to the hospital, and thankfully Mom looked good. She was lamenting that she had to be in the hospital on her birthday, but Lawrence and his family were planning a little party for her in her room for early that evening. That brightened her spirit.

I started feeling so much better when I saw and talked to her. She pointed to her arm and said it was a little sore. Her best friend had just died, and she had spent many hours on the telephone letting people know and helping her friend's family. She said her arm was sore from holding the phone up to her ear for so many hours. With just a sore arm, everyone thought she would probably go home on Saturday. They were just keeping her for observation, and I began to relax. I still wanted to stay, but Mom assured me it wasn't necessary and that she was fine. Mom loved her independence, didn't seem to be concerned, and was looking forward to my brother and his family coming in a couple of hours to celebrate her birthday.

We had made plans to be in Des Moines the next day, so we hugged Mom goodbye and drove home. My brother called me Saturday afternoon to let me know that Mom hadn't slept very well Friday night, so she was going to stay another day in the hospital. He seemed sure that she'd come home on Sunday. This was unexpected news, and I was still a bit concerned, so I called her early that evening. She was getting ready to eat supper, so we didn't talk long. She seemed tired, but said she was good and planned to go home on Sunday. I thought that sounded all right, and we said goodbye.

On Sunday afternoon, I was doing laundry and getting ready for the week, when another family member called me to report that Mom was going to stay another day as she hadn't gotten much sleep again on Saturday night. I was surprised to hear this, but felt that with no sleep, she'd be a little weak, and it was better for her to stay in the hospital one more day. She still felt fine, but was tired, so they said they would call Mom later in the evening. I thought, good, Mom would be able to rest, and I'd hear how she was later that night.

I went about the day thinking all was well and looking forward to my next update. But when I received the call Sunday evening, the news wasn't good. They said Mom sounded groggy and not herself. My intuition kicked into high gear. I saw in my mind's eye a mini-movie of a nurse walking into Mom's hospital room and giving her a pill. My intuition told me that Mom was not doing well, and I wasn't sure why. Was she not tolerating some of the medication she was being given? With no real answers, my family's concerned voices, and my intuition sounding an alarm bell, I was worried. I made the decision to pack my bags and head down to Mom's first thing in the morning. I don't see well at night and didn't want to make the three-hour drive in the dark, so that was the soonest I felt I could leave.

I was already halfway to the hospital Monday morning when my cell phone rang. It was Lawrence telling me he'd just seen Mom in the hospital. She wasn't herself at all, and he was worried. There was no way she was going home! As calmly as I could, I said, "The good news is that I'm in the car with a suitcase packed, and I'm already half-way there. The bad news is I won't be there for another hour and a half."

The next two hours were a blur. I just remember practically running down the hallway to Mom's room after I entered the hospital. I came to the nurse's station first. A nurse with a small paper cup in her hand was headed to a room. I asked her if she knew where my mom was, and she said yes, she was on her way into Mom's room to give her a pill. Yes, that's exactly what she said. Gulp! I froze for a second, as I had seen this exact vision in my mind the night before.

I asked her what the pill was. She said it was to help her relax. I said I wanted her to wait on giving it to her and probably not give it to her at all. I added that two family members had phoned me with news that Mom wasn't doing well, that she wasn't herself.

The nurse turned around and walked back to her station. It probably wasn't the first time she'd had to deal with a panicked patient's loved one who was over-the-top worried. I took a couple breaths to collect myself. When I walked into Mom's room, she was dozing. She looked up through sleepy eyes and smiled at me. I stood by her bed, took her hand, and wept.

I would find out later that mom had gotten out of her bed in the middle of the night and walked up and down the hallway as if she was lost. At the time I didn't know what was happening to her. But Mom had never taken pills for relaxing, and I wasn't sure they were helping her. People can have different reactions to the same medication. What works for some doesn't work for everyone. Later, I also read about a real issue that commonly occurs for people staying in a hospital. People can experience delirium when they are in an environment that is institutional without any of their home comforts and familiar routines. While it can happen to anyone at any age, delirium happens to 20-30% of older people in a hospital. Heads up and warning! I learned the hard way that if you have someone in the hospital, especially an older person, make sure that you try to always have someone with them, someone who knows them and loves them, to keep them grounded so they can feel as safe and comfortable in the new setting as possible.

Your intuition is a powerful gift. Listen to it. When I heard that Mom was groggy and not herself, I immediately envisioned a nurse giving her a pill. I also felt that Mom needed help. I didn't want to panic, but I felt I needed to get down there to find out what was going on. I read much later that delirium can cause dementia, and I was happy that I'd gotten down to be with Mom as soon as I could. Whether her body wasn't handling the medications she was being given or it was delirium or something else, my God-given Spiritual Communication ability summoned me to her. When you find yourself in crisis mode, you don't always have the time or the energy to track down all the details of a situation. That's when God and intuition have your back.

And things were starting to get busier and more complicated with my mom. It took all my focus and energy to stay in the moment. I had no idea how much I would rely on my ability to be open to God's Divine Intervention in the days and weeks ahead.

My intuition, my ability to sense the energy and know whether something was good or bad, was intact. When I got the report that my mom wasn't doing very well, I felt the negative energy around this situation. When I saw the vision of the nurse giving Mom a pill? I would learn years later that this is called a remote viewing. Remote viewing is "seeing" a specific occurrence that has either happened, is happening at the same time you are "seeing" it, or it will happen.

Remote viewing is another miraculous way the Holy Spirit sends important messages to us and for us. God works His miracles to provide love, protection, and guidance to help us. I was thankful and appreciative to God for equipping me with a potentially life-saving truth barometer.

How have you experienced intuition in your life?

Do you listen to it? Do you pay close attention to it, or do you dismiss it?

I would suggest that you pay attention to your intuition. Even if you are wrong, I believe that if it's at all possible to do some checking on your gut hunches, you can at least check out the situation for yourself and put your mind at ease.

CHAPTER 3

An Angel Appears

M om felt tired but was perking up after her nap, and we had a good
time catching up with each other as we talked in her room. I was
so relieved that I'd come down to be with her. I was planning to stay
overnight in her room with her until she could go home and get settled
again. Visiting hours were over in the small-town hospital. I quickly
discovered that she was the only patient in the hospital, and we joked
that she had the whole place to herself.

Mom had her supper, was settling in her bed, and getting ready to
go to sleep. Cell phones only worked in the hospital lobby, so I thought
I'd head to the lobby to call Gary and text my family with an update
on Mom. It was around 9:30 p.m. when I finished making my calls.
I was walking down the long corridor back to Mom's hospital room,
thinking about everything I would need to handle in the morning. I
closed my eyes and let out a long sigh, just trying to prepare for a night
in an uncomfortable recliner chair and hoping my mom was going to
get better.

Suddenly, to my right, I sensed someone walking next to me!

I looked over and stopped. Out of nowhere, I saw a woman next to me. I had not seen or heard her approach. I had no idea where she might have come from. She wasn't a nurse; she was in jeans and a sweater. No coat. At first, I thought, oh, she's another visitor. (It would be a long time before I would finally sort out that night in my mind, remembering there were no other patients in the hospital, and realize who she really was.)

I said, "Oh, I didn't see you!"

She smiled and said, "Is it your mother that's in the hospital?"

I said, "Yes. I just got down here today."

She nodded and said, "It's hard when your mom is ill. I took care of my mom, too."

I asked her if she knew my mom. She said she didn't know her but had heard she was in the hospital. I didn't think anything of this, because word travels fast in a small town.

Then she talked about there being so much to do with all the tasks for taking care of things both medically and financially. I agreed and told her that I had just begun to put together a list of things I needed to take care of. She asked me if I had my name on Mom's bank account. I told her I didn't. She said it would be helpful, because my mom might need me to pay her bills while she was in the hospital. She said she'd done that for her own mother, and it made things simple and easy. Otherwise, I'd have to get a court order to pay my mom's bills for her if she became medically incapacitated. I hated to think about that possibility, but I knew I needed to take care of this task. I thanked her and told her that it made a lot of sense and that I would take care of it first thing in the morning. She explained that the bank would have a form that I could pick up. I should have Mom sign it and then take it back to the bank right away. She took the time to go through each step, which I thought was so kind of her and extremely helpful to me, as the list of things that needed to be done seemed to be adding up. I was tired from the drive and beginning to feel overwhelmed.

We started to walk together again, after she explained everything. I was thanking her for her help when I saw that we were almost to the nurse's station. I looked over to say something and realized she was gone. Just disappeared. I looked down the different hallways, and there was no one around. No sounds of footsteps, doors opening or closing. I thought it was very strange. Where did she go?

It would be years before I realized what had just happened. When I'd have a chance to retrace every moment of that night. Rethink all the possibilities of the woman who had just appeared, helped me with what would turn out to be a highly important piece of information, and then—just disappeared.

I now know this was an Angel who had come in human form to assist me that night. She wasn't there to visit my mom. She didn't know my mom. I had just been in the lobby making phone calls and texting my family updates on my mom. Nobody walked into that hospital. I even asked the nurse at the station if she had seen the woman I had been walking with. She hadn't. She reminded me that Mom was their only patient, and no one else had been to visit my mom that evening but me.

This is one of my favorite Divine Intervention experiences. I now know how God sends His helpful and beautiful messengers to aid us in times of stress, loss, overwhelm, and need. As it turned out, I would need that form signed; Mom would end up being in the hospital a total of three weeks. If I hadn't gotten that form signed, I might have had to go to court to attend to her affairs.

Angels appearing as humans is, to me, one of the most beautiful examples of Divine Intervention. I've read about them over the years, and the consensus is that they try not to stand out or appear out of the ordinary, even though they can't help but appear out of the ordinary.

Do you know of an Angel appearing in your life? Or the life of someone you know?

How did you feel about it?

Were you like me, not figuring it out until much later because of overwhelming and distracting circumstances? Once I figured out who this visitor was, I began to feel how loved I was, how loved we all are. I even wonder how many other Angels have been sent down in my life who, because I wasn't aware of what was happening at the time, I missed realizing who they were.

While their aim is not to be discovered, but only to help, I feel that it would have been nice to thank her properly. Over the years, every time I think about this experience, I do thank her and Divine Guidance for watching over me. Having my mom in the hospital was such a devastating time in my life. To know that in our times of greatest need, we will be, and are, assisted in such simple and beautiful ways touches my heart and makes me feel truly loved by God and His Divine Beings.

CHAPTER 4

Eternity Arm Duet

I hurried back to my mom's hospital room after the helpful woman/Angel experience and got organized for the night as quietly as I could, as Mom's eyes were already closed. I'd be sleeping in the chair that was placed by the window in her room. It was a recliner that didn't really recline all the way. I was exhausted. The nurse had brought me a pillow and blanket. I threw the blanket over me, hoped for the best, and somehow fell asleep.

It had been a fitful night, and my neck was not happy. But daylight arrived, and I figured that soon, someone would be in to check on Mom. I closed my eyes and said a quick prayer asking for help with my mom getting her strength back so I could take her home soon.

I heard and sensed something moving to my left. I opened my eyes to see what it was. Was Mom awake?

At first, I wasn't sure what I was seeing. I could see Mom's right arm moving through the air, gliding back and forth. I sat up and put my glasses on. What I saw sent tingles through my entire body.

My mom's right arm was not only gliding back and forth through the air, but it was making a figure eight loop over and over. And she was still asleep. I sat there in shock. Not so much from what she was doing, but from what I had been doing during the last several months before Mom landed in the hospital.

Sometime in the summer, before Mom entered the hospital, I found my left arm rising of its own accord and making figure eight loops over and over. This was the exact same motion that I now observed my mom doing! The first time it happened to me, it was morning, and I lay in bed simply marveling at how my arm was moving all by itself. I was totally conscious and could have stopped it, but I felt no desire to. It felt so good. Rather glorious! I really don't know how long I watched my arm gliding back and forth in that movement, but it was probably at least two minutes. I thought, oh, it's the sign of infinity and eternity too. That is so cool. I have loved the symbol for the number eight since I was a kid.

Anyway, throughout the summer, I found my left arm moving like this infrequently, maybe once a week. Always when I was in bed. It would half surprise me for a second, then I would just observe myself and enjoy it. Sometimes it happened when I woke up in the morning. Or before I fell asleep at night. A couple of times, it happened when I was watching TV. I thought it was cool. My husband knew about it, but I didn't really mention it to anyone else. Frankly, I didn't think all that much about it, except that I was doing it periodically that summer and it felt good. A couple of times, I thought I was communing with God in some no-words-to explain-it sense.

So, you can imagine my shock that morning as I watched my mom in her hospital bed doing the Exact—Same—Thing while she was sleeping!

I quietly got out of my makeshift bed, went around to the foot of Mom's bed, and watched. It was beautiful. Her face was serene with her eyes closed, and I let myself feel the peace of this full circle—certainly Divine to me—moment.

I don't know how long I stood there. Mom must have sensed me watching her, because her eyes opened slowly, and she gave me the most Angelic look and smile, not conscious of what she had been doing. As her eyes opened, her arm slowly dropped back to the bed.

I didn't know what to call what had happened, but it had happened. It made me feel that we weren't alone. It made me feel like we were being connected in a most exciting and spiritual way. I still don't know what to call it, even though I have created categories for each of my Divine Intervention experiences. I have a category named Divine Natural Phenomena. It's a category I use when I really don't know what words to use to describe what I have just experienced. Whatever anyone wants to call this experience, I knew Mom and I were in sync and connected. What are the chances of me even being awake in time to see it? I marvel at all the spiritual synchronicities that happen in our lives. A tiny miracle happened for me that day. Both of our arms were making the same sign of Eternity. It signified to me that our bond of love was intact in this life, and it would also be intact when Mom passed on to Heaven. I was filled with such love and peace; I still cry when I think about it.

What unexplainable Divine Intervention experiences have you had in your life?

Life moves so fast most of the time that we rarely capture the most significant, sometimes unexplainable, moments of our lives. Close your eyes and let a memory of such a time come to the surface. What experiences took your breath away? Stopped you in your tracks? Were so profound that you called your wife, husband, partner, mom, dad, son, daughter, best friend, or co-worker, on the spot, so you could tell them all about it before your breathlessness faded away?

Let these questions percolate if your answers don't come right away. Don't be surprised if a couple of days or weeks down the road, when you're driving or eating lunch, something pops into your mind. Make sure you write it down as soon as you can. Let yourself go back to how you felt when the memory actually happened. Allow yourself to reconnect to all the moments you have had that felt special, hard to explain, hard to believe, even for you—the one they happened to. These are the moments that tell you unequivocally that you are connected to something greater than can be described. But it is real. It happened.

I have found that when I start focusing on the moments and experiences of Divine Intervention in my life and others' lives, I start feeling uplifted, better, less worried about the future, and even less concerned or fearful about death. That's what I want for you, and it's a big part of the reason I wrote this book.

CHAPTER 5

Mom's Near-Death Experience

It was the next morning, the second day I was in the hospital with my mom, and the sixth day of her being in the hospital. She was in better spirits, but still quite weak, and it didn't look like she was going home yet. She signed the bank form, and I promptly returned it to the bank as soon as Mom settled in for a snooze. I went to Mom's house to take care of some things like finding her checkbook and getting up to date on the status of her bills. I also had phone appointments with some of my coaching clients that afternoon, so I focused on getting everything done and planned to head back to Mom after my client calls.

Mom was awake when I got there, and we had fun talking. She seemed to be stronger, which was really good to see. I called and texted my family and Gary and gave them today's report that she was doing better even though she was still quite tired and weak.

After a rather quiet day, Mom and I had supper and settled in for the evening. Mom was sleeping by 9:00 p.m., and I had brought a book, so we were set for the night.

I'm not sure what time I fell asleep that night, but I bolted out of the recliner when I was awakened by someone turning on the light in Mom's room. I saw a flurry of movement. There were two nurses in the room attending Mom. I asked what was wrong, and they said Mom was losing fluids, and her systolic blood pressure was over 200. I knew that wasn't good. I started panicking. Was Mom going to die?

The nurses explained they were going to change the sheets and get her dry. They would try to get her warmed up and stabilized. They said I could go sit at the nurse's station. I hovered over Mom and them for a while but could feel myself getting weak. I ran to the bathroom and splashed cold water on my face, looked in the mirror, but didn't recognize myself. The look of horror and worry looking back scared me. I turned away and headed back to Mom's room.

I finally saw the time, 3:30 a.m. The nurses were walking out of Mom's room. They told me that she was resting, seemed comfortable, and that was all they could do for now. I went and looked at her. I wasn't ready for this. This wasn't part of the plan. I asked God to save her and told her she was going to be okay.

It was a nightmare of a night. I remember sitting at the nurse's station later, praying for God to save her. And if He couldn't save her, to at least spare my mother any suffering.

I felt helpless. The only thing I could do was pray. And I did. I asked God for help to get through whatever lay ahead. I asked for guidance to be able to make the best possible decisions for my mom. I asked for strength to handle anything that I would need to do. As lost as I felt that night, I did feel comfort from God's listening and grace. And, in the days ahead, that feeling never left me.

Whatever happened that night, my mom seemed like a different person the next day. I learned later that it was probably a medium level stroke. But she was alive and trying to make sense of her new situation. And I was a grateful daughter.

She seemed herself, but her words were out of order, and she spoke in very short, simple sentences. Almost like how I learned to read in first grade. Remember? Like, *See Dick run*. You could tell it really bothered her. I didn't care. I was just elated she'd lived through the night. So the next couple of days were spent de-jumbling the order of her words. I got good at it. She understood everything I said perfectly, and she knew I didn't care what order her words came out in, so we were having fun. We made a game out of trying to figure out what the heck she was trying to say. Which was typical for Mom. Anyone who knew her loved her. She was a saint in many ways to so many people. If there was fun to be had, she was all for it.

Everyone else wasn't as happy with these changes in Mom as we seemed to be, but they hadn't seen what I'd seen. Death had been a little too close that harrowing night, and the current state Mom was in—that she was alive at all—was a miracle to me. I accepted that she wasn't in perfect shape now, but she was alive. We were communicating well enough for us to understand each other, and I wasn't going to let anyone take that away from Mom or me. My role with her had changed. She was still my mama, but I had become her Mama Bear. If someone was going to try and act like there was something wrong with her because she couldn't talk perfectly, I started to growl.

Besides, I knew enough about the Divine Energy System by then to understand how important it was to be as positive as possible. Feeling good about herself would assist my mom in regaining her strength.

One afternoon, a couple of days later, Mom started talking about the man who came for her that night. "Came man. Me night," she said matter-of-factly.

Okay. I tried not to look startled. "What man came for you that night?" I asked.

"Know don't man. Light. Walk. Ready? No." She shook her head after she spoke her words slowly.

"Uh, a man, you don't know who it was, with a light, walked with you. And you weren't ready?" I deciphered.

She nodded approval.

"What weren't you ready for?"

"Die. Heaven," she said.

If this had been some game show, we would have just won two weeks at an exclusive Maui resort, all expenses paid. Including air fare.

Well, it wasn't a game show, but I'm pretty sure Mom had just shared with me that she had had a near-death experience (NDE). I put together that she had been given a choice to make, and she decided that she wasn't done living here on earth. She was given the opportunity to decide whether to continue to Heaven or turn around and come back to her life on earth. I was speechless, but so happy she'd come back. It was then I knew she had faced death, but her soul wanted to come back.

Also, because she had been so close to death, and I had witnessed it, in the back of my mind, I started preparing for her passing. I felt like God had given her that choice, and whether she lived five more days or five more years, it would be part of my mission to somehow do my best to embrace every day with her—as a gift—and yet begin to prepare for the day that would be her last. That may sound strange, but if you've faced something like this or lost someone, especially a close loved one, you probably understand what I am trying to say.

And I figured she had come back for a reason. While I didn't know what her reason or reasons were exactly, I felt that it had to be important. Important to her, her soul's journey, important to God, and very important to me and anyone else who knew and loved her.

Facing death, your own or a loved one's, seems impossible. Those who experience a near-death experience come close to physical finality. They experience a state of being that allows them to decide to transition to Heaven or to come back to earth. When Mom came back, it felt like a complete miracle to me, especially after witnessing her coming so close to dying.

I said earlier that mom was different that next day after her stroke. But it wasn't just her speech. She was lighter. How can a very lovely person become even lovelier? Well, she did. She had a smoother flow. She had so few rough edges before, but the ones she did have were buffed out. Very subtle, but recognizable to me. Nothing seemed to bother her after that. She seemed like she was floating a little. Between two worlds. This one and Heaven.

I changed, too. I was a little less rough around my own edges. Mostly about facing the unknown. And life and death. While I was still scared about my loved ones dying, I was experiencing something subtle about death that I couldn't really define; it just felt different. Maybe, by watching Mom come so close to it, it gave me a taste of acceptance. Not a big bite of acceptance, just a nibble. Even though I was raised a Christian and believed in God, Jesus, Heaven, the Holy Spirit, and the Afterlife, something shifted in me. After Mom's near-death experience, I not only believed—I now felt like I *knew* that God and Heaven were real. Because she was able to share with me what happened, and I had been five feet away wondering if she was going to live that night, I believed her. Even in her *see-Jane-run* state, I believed her.

Oh, and another thing? I asked Mom if she was scared during her near-death experience. She shook her head no.

Every time I have read about a near-death experience, the people report they were not afraid. Hmm. I can't say that I'm totally unafraid of dying. But since my Mom's NDE, let's just say I am more at peace with the idea of death.

Have you or a loved one experienced a near-death experience? What was it like? How did it change your life and the life of the person experiencing it? How do you feel about death and dying since reading about this NDE?

CHAPTER 6

ACUTE: My Five-Step System for Spiritual Communication

I was sitting in the lobby of the hospital. This was my perch each night when Mom went to sleep. It's where I would come to text and call my family and friends at the end of each long day in the hospital. It was the only place my cell phone got reception there. The lights were out in the lobby, and the front door was locked. The outdoor lights coming in through the glass and the lights that were on at the far ends of the hallways gave enough light for me to see. It felt safe and peaceful there.

Tonight, the custodian was busy emptying waste baskets and pushing the dirt from the day's footsteps. I had seen him almost every night during my end-of-the-day lobby routine. We had always spoken politely to each other and silently respected each other's tasks. I was in the middle of a text when I saw him approach quietly.

"I hate to bother you," he said tentatively as he cleared his throat.

"Oh, hello!" I said, a little surprised when I looked up. "It's no bother." I waited as I looked up at his face.

"Well, I've been watching you. And you're here each night…"

"Yes," I wasn't sure where this was going.

"…Well, I keep feeling like I'm supposed to talk with you," he finally admitted. "And I wondered if I could ask you a question."

Interestingly, while he was talking, I got the feeling that I was supposed to talk with him!

"Sure!" I said.

"Well, I am a Christian. And I have been attending conferences where they have speakers. I am enjoying them, but…." his voice trailed off.

"You want to know what's next, right?" I asked him. "You feel you are ready to serve God in more direct ways, and you might like to help in some way at these conferences, but you are hesitating because you're unsure."

He said, "That's exactly what I've been thinking about!" surprised that I knew and was making this relatively easy for him to converse about.

I answered, "Yes, you are ready to take the next steps, in whatever way you are comfortable. You might want to find people who you are standing or sitting next to and ask them questions about their faith journey, or you could share some thoughts about what the last speaker spoke about that was significant to you. You might also approach your own minister or the people who oversee the conferences and share your desire to serve with them and ask them what ideas they might have. You also might want to ask God directly. That's the beautiful thing about our spiritual journeys; we evolve when it's the right time for us, and it's normal to develop a desire to serve God in different ways that are more fulfilling for you."

He said, "Thank you so much! I feel so much better, and I think I could do some of the things you talked about! Uh, how do you know these things? How did you know what I was trying to ask you before I asked you?"

"Well, you know how you felt like you were supposed to talk with me?" I asked.

"Yes," he said as if he was wondering what I would say next.

"Well, it's the same for me. It's like I pick up your soul's energy signal and, somehow, I connect with it. I've been able to do this effortlessly since I was a kid. It's our God-given intuitive ability that we all have from birth. But so many people ignore it or don't use it very often, and when they do use it, they don't even realize it! You were probably taking your own ability for granted when you felt like you were supposed to talk with me."

"Yes—uh—I believe—that's right!" he exclaimed, as if he had just had a wonderful ah-hah moment of recognizing what I said was true for him.

"Maybe the only difference between us in this instance is that I have almost always valued my 'knowings,' and I have honored them. I didn't drop them when I was a kid, like I think most people do. I noticed them, was happy I had them, and used them every day! So, after using them daily for fifty-four years, I've practiced a lot," I chuckled.

He said, "Wow! You've given me a lot to think about."

"Kind of like discovering a gift that you never knew you had, but it was always there for you, right?" I smiled as I asked him.

"Exactly," he exclaimed. "But now that I know this, I really don't know what to do about it."

"Enjoy it! Use it! Recognize when you are already utilizing it unconsciously. Give thanks for it. God gives us so much, but so many of us focus on our troubles and issues. We all have issues, but I have learned to give them up to God. The next thing I know, I feel that my prayers are answered. I either know what to do about something, or I let it go and see what God and all His Helpers are going to do. If I'm supposed to do something, I usually get some message, an inkling or hunch, about it, and then I can proceed. Living on earth is a bit of a bronco ride sometimes, so that's why I rely on God's communication system. I'm always amazed when people tell me they don't know what I'm talking about," I shrugged.

He stood there for a minute in wonderment. Then he smiled. Like he had just been told the best secret ever. He thanked me, shook his head, appeared lost in his new thoughts, and got back to his sweeping.

What is your experience with your Intuition?

What were your thoughts about Intuition before you read this story?

What are your thoughts now?

What are your favorite intuition experiences that you or someone you know has had?

What else do you want to know about your Intuition?

This example of Divine Intervention that I experienced that night was the perfect example of someone focusing on their spiritual journey and wanting help and support with the next step. This man created his spiritual desire, sensed vibrationally that I could help him with it, and I sensed and read the energetic frequency of his soul's desire. He was experiencing distinct feelings and knowings and trusted them enough to approach me. This is one of the biggest issues for people in learning how to use our Spiritual Communication System. When I polled some friends recently, they all admitted they don't always follow their intuitive inklings. While the man who approached me wasn't completely aware of what he was doing or how he was doing it, he trusted his energetic vibrations enough to act and approach me. We didn't know each other. We had barely said more than a couple of words of greetings to each other before that conversation.

I helped him understand what had just happened, and then he was able to process it and become more aware of his ability to communicate spiritually. Because we *were* communicating spiritually with each other, and rather effortlessly! That's what's wonderful about intuition and Divine Intervention. This incredible system that was created for us allows us to communicate with other humans who have left this world, but it also works with people who are alive. We all have had the experience of thinking of someone and then they call or somehow contact us. You have free will to think it's nothing, but I am comfortable in knowing that this system works from my own and others' real-life experiences. That's the acid test for me.

When I started working with Light Workers, those who desired to serve God and those on their Spiritual journeys, I created an easy and doable Five-Step ACUTE System to help people focus and get back in touch with their Spiritual Communication System. Again, Divine Intervention was at play. I wrote out what I thought were the steps of this process:

1. *Accept* that spiritual communication is real.
2. *Claim* it for yourself and start using it.
3. *Utilize* the tools and strategies, such as praying, meditating, and appreciating, to activate, expand, and strengthen your intuitive abilities.
4. *Trust* your feelings and the messages and signs you are receiving.
5. *Enjoy* the process and journey of Spiritual Communication.

After I'd written out the steps, suddenly, I got the tingles as I was directed to notice the first letter of the first words of each step. Those letters spelled ACUTE. I had just been guided to notice an acronym which would help this tool serve people better by making it easy to remember. It felt like another Divine gift to have this easy word to help people remember the steps so they could easily and quickly utilize, practice, and get comfortable using their Spiritual Communication System.

Here's a more detailed explanation of the ACUTE System:

- **Step one. A** stands for **Accepting** that you are a spiritual being and designed by our Creator/God to be able to get all sorts of messages from God, the Angels, other humans in the physical world, and your deceased loved ones in the Spiritual Realm.

- **Step two.** <u>C</u> <u>stands for</u> **Claiming** your built-in Spiritual Communication System. It's one thing to accept that it's true, but it's another matter entirely to claim it for yourself, as part of who you are. Claiming is such an important step. When you claim it, you plug yourself into the Divine Energy System we live in, like plugging into an electrical socket. You are now ON!

- **Step three.** <u>U</u> <u>stands for</u> **Utilizing** simple tools and strategies to help you focus, to enable you to recognize Spiritual language by spending time doing the best activities to help activate and strengthen your ability to use your Divine intuition system. It's like weight training. To strengthen your muscles, you've got to move them, practice your exercises, and train your muscles to become stronger. Those who have spent time in a hospital bed or at home on bed rest for a stretch of time quickly learn they must keep moving or their muscles become weak. Like our body's muscle system, our Spiritual Communicating abilities can become rusty if ignored and not used.

To strengthen your Spiritual Communication System, you've got to spend time learning. You need to practice feeling it in order to strengthen it, to become more aware of it, and to recognize when it's happening. Most people use this system every day, but they aren't aware they are using it, like the janitor. Some will even deny they are using it, which is even more confusing.

I love teaching clients the many tools and strategies to strengthen and expand their abilities to communicate spiritually. (See Appendix 2 for more tools and strategies.) However, *praying*, asking God's help, *meditating,* and *appreciating* are the three most important and impactful tools you can use.

Praying opens the communication line. You are talking to God (with the Spiritual Communication System) and looking for His answers (from the Spiritual Communication System). I am always amazed when I talk to people about praying being the most fundamental form of spiritual communication. I sometimes hear that spiritual communication isn't possible and doesn't exist. But after I ask them if they pray, and they say, "Of course I pray," I remind them that when they pray, they are participating in Divine Spiritual Communication. Praying is something that most of us learned how to do when we were small children. If a person is open, awake, and aware, they will connect the dots quickly. Chances are if they are closed-minded and cynical, they will angrily disagree. I learned a long time ago that everyone has the right to decide for themselves, and I'm okay with where people land.

When you seek answers, you need to take time to be quiet, sit, and practice "sensing" what messages you may be getting. If you have constant noise and activity in your life and you aren't used to using your Spiritual Communication System, it might take some practicing to be able to perceive when you are getting messages. With time and practice, you will get there.

You need to become open and aware when you get an idea, an inkling, or a hunch about something. Instead of ignoring these God Answers and Godsends, as I sometimes like to call them, you need to pay attention to them, be willing to see how you feel about them, and how you resonate with them. There is no doubt in my mind that you are receiving plenty of messages, but the problem is, you are probably ignoring, discounting, and taking most of them for granted without realizing the power of these messages and where they really come from. This lack of being able to *perceive* is where most people fail to receive their Divine messages.

Meditating helps you reach a neutral state and let go of any resistance you may be experiencing. Resistance, or any negative energy, stops the flow of spiritual communication. But when you are quiet, relaxed, and open to aligning with your Spiritual Self, you can focus on this Spiritual Communication frequency.

When you are in a meditative state, you are energetically aligned. Some say you only need to meditate fifteen minutes a day. I encourage you to experiment with how you meditate and for how long. I meditate anywhere from fifteen minutes up to two hours each day. This usually happens in the morning, while I'm still in bed. I usually wake up between 5 and 6 a.m. and don't have to get moving that early, so I lay there and meditate. Sometimes I am so relaxed I fall back to sleep, and that's ok. I don't stress about the exact amount of time I meditate. Meditation is a great investment of my time, as I believe that it has a direct and positive influence on my health, peace, and happiness, but it also helps me focus on my spiritual frequency, so I am more aware and apt to receive the Divine messages I'm being given.

You can utilize mediums to get a reading, but imagine being able to receive and read your own Divine messages daily. That is the ultimate gift that is always available to you.

Appreciating is the act of seeing the benefit in something. When you appreciate something, you find ways to see its merit and how it is beneficial. Taking the positive approach to everything is often discounted and ridiculed, but it is one of the best ways for your life to work better and for you to quickly become masterful with using our Divine Spiritual Communication System. Having appreciation quickly sends a "yes" message that brings your desires into reality.

Even when things are going wrong for you, or you seem to be making a lot of bad choices, if you can appreciate what you are learning, you will change your direction so things will go better for you. The biggest mistake I see myself and others make in our lives is when we beat ourselves up when things don't turn out the way we wanted them to. I've been practicing for many years to stay positive and learn to appreciate everything. I strive to learn quickly and choose better as soon as I can. Appreciating and staying positive no matter what can make the difference between a good day and a bad day. Life is made up of each of your days. If you want to have a better life, appreciating more in your everyday life will do wonders.

- **Step Four. T** stands for **Trusting** yourself that you will get the information you need and be able to decipher it. The more you trust that God and His Spiritual Realm know what they are doing, the more you can relax and just open yourself to receiving what is given to you. Trusting is really important, because when you trust, you are emitting a higher frequency that allows messages to come through more easily. If you doubt that you are going to be able to receive messages, you close off the frequency that allows it to happen. You are not *making* this happen, you are *allowing* it to happen. Big difference. You can relax, stay open, and trust God and the Spiritual Realm to know what they are doing.

- **Step Five. E** stands for **Enjoying** the process. When you open yourself to Spiritual Communication, as you become open, relaxed, and enjoy the process of receiving the information, you will start to realize how effortless it really is. If you are open and aware, you will receive the messages. If you are in a negative state, you will probably close off your ability to allow the connection. If you are relaxed and enjoying the process, you will have more success. It's such a wonderful thing to know—God loves us so much that He wasn't going to send us off to earth without a spiritual, connecting lifeline of love, protection, and guidance.

This simple five-step ACUTE System gives you a quick process to reconnect to your spiritual self and strengthen and expand your ability to perceive, receive, and decipher God's most helpful messages. (Refer to Appendix 2 for a summary of the ACUTE system for easy reference and to find more tools to help you strengthen your ability to connect to the Divine Spiritual Communication System.)

CHAPTER 7

Dad's Spirit Visits

Mom spent three weeks in the hospital. She was still weak, couldn't do the physical therapy required, but was doing okay with her speech. Personally, I thought she needed rest and a feeling of normalcy in her life. It was time to make some decisions on what was next.

Maybe she'd like to come live with Gary and me or find a facility close to us? (We lived three hours away from her.) Staying in her own home was not recommended, as we knew about others' nightmarish experiences with caretakers not always showing up and not having back-up care during harsh Iowa winters.

Remember when I said that Mom was so wonderful through all of this? Well, she knew what she wanted and was happy about it. She said, "I'm going to live at the nursing home in town. I have volunteered there for so long that I know everyone. I will feel comfortable there, and I want my kids to live their own lives. I don't want you to have to take care of me!"

So off she went and bravely accepted her new place of residence. When I approached her about not driving because of the strokes, here's what she said, "I am so grateful that I have been able to drive for as long as I have and without having any accidents or hurting anyone. I'm very okay with giving up driving!"

She settled in, played the piano for their church services, enjoyed her tablemates at meals, attended their various planned activities, both inside and outside the facility, took an almost daily afternoon nap, and confided to me that now that she was a lady of leisure, she really didn't miss cooking or writing out checks to pay her bills anymore! Mom was a peach; she knew how to bloom where she was planted.

Life for everyone got back to almost normal, and I was able to make sure she was well tended through phone calls with her caregivers and family members trading off weekend visits.

Mom, Gary, and I agreed that Gary and I should go to Florida for the winter as planned. We would fly home if there were any emergencies.

That winter, Mom and I ended up having priceless phone calls several times a week about her life growing up, before she married Dad, and her philosophies on subjects we had never really had time to talk about before. I felt I couldn't get enough time with her, and she loved every minute of answering my questions about her life experiences and sharing stories about all the relatives. Mom was the vital family connector of our clan. She was the matriarch and took this role happily and seriously. She might forget what she had for lunch yesterday, but the beloved stories she knew from all the family's lives, both on her and our dad's sides, were solid and never in question.

I approached the subject of planning her funeral. She was now eighty-seven, continued to have mild strokes periodically, and I sensed we were on borrowed time with her. She thought that planning it together was a splendid idea, and we had a lot of fun planning the details, with her favorite hymns, having the full choir, if possible, and even what she wanted the minister to do. I always say that I love a woman who knows what she wants. And Mom didn't disappoint.

That winter, talking with Mom all those hours was special. My dad had crossed over nine years earlier. Talking with Mom about both her and Dad had me thinking about him frequently.

One day, I had just finished watching the TV show, *Long Island Medium*. This episode was about a woman's father who had come through and provided healing for his daughter in a reading that Theresa Caputo had given (Season 1, Episode 7, 2011). It was sad and amazing. As I turned the TV off when the show was over, I started thinking about my dad.

Suddenly, I felt a presence at my left side. I was a little taken aback and wasn't sure what was going on. As I sat there wondering what was happening, suddenly, this energy started sending me thoughts and communicating with me. I recognized it as my dad's spirit. I couldn't believe it. He was telling me he was sorry for certain events in his life, and he now realized how they had affected me and others in our family. I couldn't believe my ears. Dad had anger issues, and throughout his life, I never heard him apologize to anyone. I started crying. Part of me was in disbelief about what was happening, but it was undeniable. He was talking to me like he was sitting right next to me. He asked me for forgiveness. I found myself talking to him through my tears. It felt like my child self was telling him how hard and devastating it had been for me, how much my feelings were hurt, and how I felt like I had never gotten over it.

He apologized over and over and allowed me to wail, whine, and lament about how awful it all had been and still was for me.

I couldn't see him, but I sensed him hanging his head. I lectured him. I slammed him. He took it and said he deserved it all.

I don't know how long this all went on. Maybe ten or fifteen minutes. When I was done and had nothing more to yell at him about, I became silent. We sat there together in that silence. Finally, he said, *"I will wait for as long as it takes and hope that someday you will forgive me."*

And then, I felt the shift. With all that emotion processed and drained out of me, and with him listening and admitting his wrong ways, I was able to transform. I was still mad at him, but I wanted to forgive him, so I did.

I told him that even though I forgave him, I would probably still be mad at him, and I didn't know if that would ever change. I loved him, but I felt I had lost so much because of his behavior. I felt like I was somewhere between four and thirteen years old in my thinking and processing during this experience.

He communicated to me that he could understand how I felt, and he could accept it all on my terms. He said that he was trying to make amends with me and the rest of our family now that he was on the Other Side.

Through the years, my visits with my dad have become more often and more peaceful. I still yell at him occasionally, but he has become the dad I always wanted when he was alive. I still cry about it all, but his contacting me from Heaven has been a miracle of love and connection that I never thought I would have, and I thank God for this.

Do you have any relationships with people who have crossed over who you wish you could reconcile with? I think we have all had relationships in our lives that have been disappointing, or perhaps we have some other unfinished business where we wish we could have another chance to make things better, or maybe we never got to say goodbye. Well, the people that die feel the same way. Once they cross over, they try to evolve and improve where they failed on earth.

I have transformed my own life through communications from more evolved loved ones' spirits from the Other Side, and I am most grateful. It seemed like Heaven had helped my dad reform into the kind and loving being I'd sometimes seen on earth but had always wished he could have been like more of the time. I was so relieved to meet my dad in this better state. It helped heal my broken heart, let me forgive him, and gave us both peace.

We come here to earth to learn our lessons and evolve spiritually. Some of us make a big mess of things when we're on earth. While no one is perfect, there are people who get stuck in their weaknesses and fear and don't really evolve during their time here.

And it's no wonder. I refer to earth as a real rodeo. Lots of trying and getting bucked off. Some of us get our hearts broken so many times, we can't get over or through it very well, and we cause suffering to others and ourselves.

And then there are our spiritual lessons. How does a person learn compassion? By learning how to love hard-to-love people. While I don't always like or understand why things are so difficult for people, difficult times can sharpen our abilities to become more loving and compassionate. The more challenging the training, the better the athlete.

Nobody ever said living on earth was easy, and it certainly isn't for the faint of heart. But I do know that the opportunity to learn spiritual lessons is part of our work here in the physical world. And some lessons are easier than others. But souls are designed to want to evolve, so it's in our nature to be challenged because the reward can be sweet. While life can be complex and hard to figure out sometimes, I have learned there is value in everything. When I focus on finding the gifts, even in my most challenging experiences, my pain eases, and I start to feel better.

I continue to learn my lessons, both easy and difficult, and trust that God knows what He's doing even when I may not understand what's going on. That's where our trust and faith serve us well.

CHAPTER 8

Mom Dies

Do you ever think your mother is going to die? Well, I didn't. But she did.

To me, my mom was like the Energizer Bunny. She just kept going.

Mom was fully engaged with life while in the nursing home. She had straightened out her earlier speech issues and was back to conversing with anyone and everyone. She knew all the residents, and she knew about their lives. When I'd come to see her, we'd always take a few minutes and walk up and down the hallways saying hello to as many people as we could. She was a deliverer of cheer everywhere she went and left people uplifted.

I went down to see her the weekend before Memorial Day weekend. She had just gotten a roommate and was excited about having a new friend to talk to. When I arrived, she was busy showing her the lay of the land. They were like two schoolgirls enjoying each other's company, and I was happy for them.

Mom was also excited because she was helping plan her 70th high school class reunion that would take place the following weekend. She had been calling everyone and setting up most of the arrangements for the last several months.

We had such a great visit together that weekend. When I left to return home, I marveled at how vibrant Mom was.

She had plans to visit her parents' and grandparents' graves with my brother on Monday, since she would be tied up with her high school classmates on the upcoming Memorial Day weekend. They had a wonderful day visiting the graves and having lunch with some of the cousins that lived in the area.

The nurse told me later that when the nurse's aide came into Mom's room to say goodnight that night, and give Mom her pain pill, Mom looked a little distant.

She asked, "Ethel, are you okay?"

Mom nodded yes and murmured, "Mm-hmm."

When the aide asked Mom what time it was, Mom looked at her watch and said, "Four, three, two...."

They called my brother first. Then he called me. "Mom has had a stroke, and it's bad," he said.

I said, "How bad?"

He didn't really know. He said, "I think you need to call the hospital."

When I talked with the person caring for my mother, she told me Mom had the stroke at the nursing home, and they had transported her to the hospital. I told the woman, "Please level with me. I'm three hours away, and I need you to tell me, as best as you can, in your experience, what are we dealing with?"

She said in an even tone, slowly, "Your mother has had a massive life-ending stroke. She's alive, but not coherent. Usually, when this happens, they are gone within twenty-four hours, if not before."

Her words felt final but true. I thanked her. The minutes were ticking by, and I only knew one thing. I didn't know how long my mother would be alive, but I knew I was going to do everything in my power to get down there as fast as humanly possible.

I'd packed funeral clothes and left them down at Mom's house when she'd been in the hospital eight months earlier. But they were winter clothes, and it was now spring. So I packed spring visitation and funeral clothing and threw everything I thought I would need together as I called our family. Gary and I arrived at the hospital around 3:00 in the morning. My brother, Lawrence, was there. We hugged but said very little. We were heartbroken. Gary and I followed Lawrence into the hospital.

They had brought in a bed for us so we could lie down next to her. I was so tired; I was grateful for the thoughtfulness of the hospital staff. I looked into my mom's face and began to feel the finality of it all. I talked to her softly and touched her face and hands. I watched her as I was in the bed next to hers. I was devoid of thoughts. I didn't know what to think, so I didn't. I just lay there and watched. I felt heavy. I felt her presence in the room, and it felt light. But it didn't feel like she was in her body but rather that she was free of it.

My brother needed some relief and left for a while. Maybe to have breakfast. I never asked him where he went. There just seemed so little reason to talk. Around noon, I realized I was getting weak and needed to eat something. The nurses said the cafeteria didn't have anything, as we had missed the cutoff to order. I didn't want to leave her, but Gary and I needed a break, too. The nurses assured me they would call me if there were any changes. We were only five minutes away from the downtown cafe, so I agreed to go.

Before I went, I stood at the foot of her bed. I told her that she could let go if she wanted to. That I was proud of her life, proud to be her daughter, and would always love her. That she had lived an amazing life, and that she could take her final bow.

We had finished lunch and were two minutes away from the hospital when I received the call that she was gone. I felt so disappointed and forlorn. But the nurses assured me that this is often how it goes. They said it's like the person wants to spare their family the burden of being there when they die, and they also have a harder time letting go when their loved ones are around them.

There was nothing to do but accept it. I had already surrendered to and been in a different world for the last eight months. A world that Mom had been in only precariously. A world that was filled with staying on alert, with anchoring myself to the present moment. I hadn't thought too far ahead. I couldn't. I think Mom and I both knew that any day in those eight months could have been her last.

One memory I had after she died was of a conversation earlier in the winter. Mom said she was afraid to die of a heart attack. She was afraid of the pain, as she had had a heart attack several years earlier and remembered how painful it had been.

Without thinking, I said, "You are not going to die from a heart attack. I'm not sure how you will die, but I'm clear you will not have any pain."

She looked at me with surprise and said, "Really?"

I said, "Really!"

While I was a bit surprised myself by what I had just said, I strongly felt it was true. By that time, I'd had a lifetime of knowing things that I didn't really know how I knew. Besides, at the time, it was what Mom needed to hear. If I could take one worry away from her, even if I couldn't explain how I knew such things, I was fine with it. Mom accepted my premonition for her and seemed at ease about the idea of her death.

So as devastated as I felt that she had died, the one consolation I had was that she had not been in any pain. I said another silent prayer of thanksgiving for the granting of this Holy Ask that I had requested over and over since she had been in the hospital eight months ago.

So, what was ahead? Certainly a new world. One without my mom. Or at least without her smiling face.

As I write this almost ten years after Mom's death, I think back to the night of her first hospital stay, when her blood pressure was over 200 and fluids were flowing from her body, not knowing if she would live through the night. I remember that even with her slow and mixed-up speaking ability that next morning, she was still my mom, and I was determined to enjoy every moment I could with her. I surprised myself and everyone around us when I could understand almost everything she was trying to say and never felt annoyed, embarrassed, or inconvenienced. In fact, we enjoyed ourselves immensely, and we were just happy to be together.

Hmmm. Were those last months we had together preparing me, in some strange and perfect way, for her actual spiritual transition to the Other Side? Where I couldn't see her or hear her in the normal human way. Where we weren't communicating like we had before, but we were communicating. I could still feel her presence and her essence whenever I wanted to. I couldn't see her, but I could see my memory of her. Whenever I thought of her, or talked to her silently or out loud, I did feel like she was there and listening. And she talked to me, too, just in a different way.

What is the relationship like between you and your deceased loved ones?

Do you feel, like I do now, that you understand more and more that our spirit lives on into eternity and that our loved ones are fully capable of still being in our lives after they cross over, just in a different way?

I have talked to friends who have lost loved ones. They describe experiences similar to mine. I think it's about the love bond that is created. The bond of love and the essence of a person never leave you.

That is how I feel now about all of those I have known, loved, and cared about who have transitioned to Heaven. They are still in my life, just in a different form. This has given me such relief and peace as I continue through my life.

CHAPTER 9

Selling Mom's House—Twice

Mom died May 22, 2012. It was now July. We had spent two weekends in June going through Mom's house to start sorting, dividing up what we would keep and what to let go of. Our family had agreed that we should try to sell the house, hopefully before the coming winter.

At the end of June, during one of these weekends at Mom's house, Gary and I had gone downtown to the Village Cup and Cakes to get some lunch. Everyone frequented this café, as Sonia Stookesberry was the mastermind baker, and her recipes were hard to resist. I was telling Gary I had no idea how to sell Mom's house. And how was I going to do it being three hours away? I was exhausted from going through just part of the house and realizing how much stuff we still had to go through. I was weary, both mentally and physically, and I kept trying to power through all that had to be done.

I said rather loudly, "God, I need help with this! I have no idea how to get Mom's house sold!"

Suddenly, John, the other half of the John and Sonia Stookesberry duo, owners of the café at the time, came up to me and said, "I overheard you talking, and I have an idea for you!"

I was all ears. He told me if it were him, he'd just go to the hardware store, buy a big sign and a marker, write "For Sale" with my cellphone number on it, and put it out in the front lawn.

I looked at Gary and said, "That sounds so simple and easy! Let's go do that right now!"

We all laughed about this perfect solution. Once again, and as had happened so many times in my life, I was saying thank you to a human Angel and God for answering my prayer so quickly.

I know that Mom loved this story too, watching from Heaven, as she knew and had been friends with John and Sonia for years. In fact, Mom gave their son, Jay, piano lessons while he was growing up. Jay was a natural (his mom, Sonia, is also a multi-talented pianist and musician), and he excelled. Mom invited Jay to perform his music throughout the years at her annual student piano recitals. In a recent conversation with them all, I found out that Jay is married, an elementary school music teacher certified in both singing and instrumental learning, gives private piano lessons, and tunes pianos, as well. What a full circle moment to hear from these wonderful people and to learn how they had impacted each other's lives. I feel that Mom's gifts and love of music lives on in so many people who she touched. And it was healing to me, even after ten years since my mom had passed, to talk with her friends and hear these stories.

As we drove away from Mom's house that night, Mom had a new addition to her lawn. And I had another human Angel experience to marvel about with wonder. We left the sign in the front yard and prayed for the best. Little did I know at the time what a Godsend John's help would be.

A couple of days later, I got a Divine inkling that I was supposed to go down to Mom's again and that I would be selling the house. I wasn't too happy about this, as my birthday was the next day, followed by the Fourth of July. Really? Is this what I really want to be doing on my birthday and a holiday?

I tried to ignore and shake off this vibe I was getting. However, by midafternoon, it was consuming my every thought. I couldn't get rid of it. By that time in my life, I'd had enough inklings, and it always turned out to be important that I follow them.

"Okay!" I said, "You win." So the next morning, I drove the three hours down to my mom's house, following a Divine premonition that was interfering with my schedule. About an hour into the drive, my cellphone rang. It was my high school friend Russell Jarvis asking me if we were selling Mom's house. I told him, "Yes!"

He said, "I know who might want to buy it!"

Turns out his sister, Jeanie, had moved back home and was looking for a house for herself. He said she wanted to look at it right away. "Bingo!" I thought.

I told him to tell her that I would be there in a couple of hours, and if she wanted to meet me there, she could.

So a while after I'd arrived at Mom's house, his sister popped in with their mom, and I gave them the tour. Jeanie loved it. She said she wanted it and was ready to write me a check on the spot.

I was a bit in shock. This was going so fast that I could hardly keep up with what was happening.

I slowed things down a bit and thought we needed to create a contract and get things done legally. Also, it was in Jeanie's best interest to have it inspected.

While that was in the works, three more people stopped in while I was there and wanted to see the house. Christie Daugherty, one of my older sister's high school classmates stopped in. She thought it would be the perfect house for someone in her family. I couldn't believe what was happening. It was like I'd scheduled an open house without doing anything but putting a sign in Mom's yard (thanks again, John) and following my Divine nudges.

In those four days, I'd received additional phone calls, and I collected a total of six names of people who might want Mom's house—and I had a down payment from Russell's sister. By this time, I was annoyed at myself for gnashing my teeth over the timing of the premonition and promptly apologized to God. I was learning when your Spiritual team is working hard in the background to help you, you have access to the entire Spiritual Realm, if need be, and I needed to be a lot more receptive and appreciative.

Within the next three weeks, still trying to get the contract completed, I was working at my desk when the phone rang.

It was Russell's sister, Jeanie. Their father had died suddenly the week before, which I knew. What I didn't know was that Jeanie decided not to move home after all. Well, a lot can happen in a couple of weeks.

By this time, I was thinking, "Here we go again!" Nearing August, I was getting a bit worried. I was also getting busier at work and had a conference coming up. At that point, I let go of focusing on selling the house, even though there was something gnawing at the back of my mind.

Another month went by. I'd just got back from my conference, so that was off my plate, and I could refocus on Mom's house.

I had kept the list of six people who had shown interest in Mom's house a couple of months prior. There was something about that list that was calling my name. I decided to contact the people on it again. After calling each one, they all said they were no longer interested.

I was going to Mom's house again, to continue the clearing out and cleaning of the house, and I kept getting a feeling about one of the people on the list. I woke up the next day with clarity.

Christie's name kept coming to me. The next morning, I realized what the new information was. The person who was supposed to buy the house was *her*, not one of her family members. I called her right away and asked her to stop over if she had time. She said she would that evening.

When I met her at the door that early evening, I said, "Guess who is supposed to buy the house?"

She said, "Who?"

I said, "You!"

She looked at me startled and then started laughing.

I had her come in, look around again, and said, "Christie, this house is perfect for you. I know you kept talking about how perfect it would be for who you had in mind, but you are the one who looked at it and fell in love with it."

I then shared that every time I pictured the buyer in my mind, it kept coming back to her. We'd had a couple of buyers continue to have interest, but they wanted us to lower the price, which I didn't want to do. These people had also mentioned they were planning to rent Mom's house out. That depressed me, and I knew that Mom wouldn't want that either.

Suddenly, Christie had a new sparkling energy about her. She was excited and started talking about what she liked about it and what she planned to do with it. She was getting me excited.

I said to her, "Well, what's it going to be? Are you going to buy this honey of a house?"

And, she said, "YES!!"

And that's how I sold Mom's house—twice.

I had a conversation with Christie recently, and she told me that after she had first seen Mom's house, she really did start to feel like she wanted the house for herself. Feelings like these do matter. They are made up of a vibrational energetic frequency that is magnetically powerful. We are all fully capable of reading the frequencies of this vibrational magnetic energy. I believe that I was picking up on her feelings, her vibrational energy frequency, and we were connecting with each other spiritually throughout the process of selling Mom's house.

Christie also shared with me that the next summer, after she bought Mom's house, she was doing some painting on the outside of the house. She happened to look up and see two women standing together with their arms linked up on the hill in the backyard. For a couple of seconds, she spiritually saw my mother and Grandma Emily Morrow, the two women who had lived in the home that was now hers. She recognized my mom and spiritually knew that the other woman was my grandma in this vision. They were looking at her with pleased expressions on their faces. They were sending her a message. She sensed that the message was: they were happy that the house went to someone with qualities similar to theirs. A woman who dedicated herself to service to others, someone with a strong work ethic, good-heartedness, and a love of God. I know Christie, and all these qualities describe her perfectly.

Christie's story of her Divine Intervention experience after she bought the house warmed my heart. She had experienced something sacred and filled with love and purpose, even though she had forgotten about it until that moment when we were talking.

We all, many times, forget our wonderful Divine Intervention moments in the continual unfolding of our days and lives. As I have done for this book and my own life, I invite you to consider writing down your own Divine Intervention moments so you have access to them and can refer to them as you marvel about all that is this life and appreciate the many Divine blessings you have received.

This is a story that touches my heart in so many ways. I now can only imagine that while I was working on selling the house, my mom and grandma were probably in on it. This is a lesson for us all. Our loved ones are part of our Spiritual team and will forever be in our corner and working behind the scenes to help us in ways we may never know. I felt privileged to learn of this story that Christie shared, and it filled me with awe, gratitude, and love.

I can't tell you how many times in my life I've gotten a premonition, a feeling so strong it's undeniable. Sometimes it's a warning about something negative that might be happening, so I can watch out for it. Other times it's telling me of something positive in order to help me.

Whether we call this form of Divine Intervention a premonition or just intuition, I have found that it's usually an important message. I always try to listen carefully and follow through on whatever the feelings are telling me to do, and I encourage you to do the same.

In this case, it guided me through the whole process of selling my mom's house. Something that I wanted and needed help with, as I didn't feel confident in my own ability to know what I was doing. That's where your intuition can come in so beautifully, and Divine Intervention saves the day! My intuition is almost always spot on. Even when I'm not sure exactly what's going to happen next. When I feel a Divine alert, I pay attention. I ask, "What is this about?" Usually, I tend to check in to find out if the feeling continues to be strong. If I can't seem to shake it, then I don't keep trying to. I go with it and take the best action I can as soon as I can.

And, how about the human Angel who helped me get the ball rolling with the idea of putting the sign in Mom's yard? Never underestimate the power of another person, whether it's someone you know or even a person you don't know very well, coming in and saving the day. When I take a minute and realize that we're all in this game of life together, and there are so many good people willing to share a good idea or physically help you in some way, it gives me joy and peace. Sure, I could have probably thought of it myself, but remember, I had just lost my mom a month before, we were undertaking a huge job, I was three hours away from home, distracted, and living out of a suitcase. Besides, I usually have a lot more fun when others start joining in on the problem solving. It's a relief when I know I don't have to figure out everything by myself. Letting my Divine Partner and my spiritual team lead the way usually brings me into a better situation, with better results than I could have created by myself.

What situations have you been in where you paid attention to a Divine inkling, nudge, or premonition warning you of something, either positively or negatively?

How does your intuition work with and for you?

Do you pay attention, listen, and act, or do you ignore it?

What did this chapter prompt you to remember?

Part II

Broken Open—Grief and Gifts

CHAPTER 10

My Grandparents and Queenie

The first part of September, Gary and I were on our way to visit some of our grandkids. I was still working on finishing up Mom's estate and had been thinking about Mom's parents, Grandpa and Grandma Morrow, and how Mom was now with them in Heaven. It brought me some solace that they were now together. But it also reminded me of how much I missed them all.

I had such wonderful grandparents and loved them so much. Grandpa died when I was ten, and Grandma died when I was nineteen. Now, at age fifty-five, I marveled at how much time had gone by. I thought of my grandpa often and thought of Grandma every day since she'd passed. I visualized their farm and how much fun I always had when I went to stay with them.

They made everything magical and special, as only grandparents can. I liked to go with Grandma on her morning chores of gathering eggs from the chickens and feeding dry oatmeal to the huge goldfish in the windmill's water trough. And on the way, we'd pet the barn cats and greet Grandpa and his black and white border collies. We usually couldn't pet Grandpa's dogs, because they were working dogs. They were highly trained by him for sheep herding, and Grandpa had to give us permission to pet them.

Living down in southeast Iowa, a lot of farmers raised sheep, as well as other livestock. Every year, the community had a Sheep Empire Day with a full parade. One year, Grandpa drove his shiny blue pickup truck in the parade. I loved riding in the back, waving and throwing candy, while his two border collies expertly herded a dozen of his sheep in front of us.

He was a strict, no-nonsense man, born in County Donegal, Ireland. He had the brogue, and I loved to hear him talk. But he was a man of very few words. He whistled. He whistled more than he talked. He'd come to the States during the Irish Potato Famine and found his way to Iowa working as a farm manager. When WWI broke out, he joined the army to fight for his new country and fought in the trenches of the Argonne Forest in France, even though he was exempt from mandatory military service. After the war, he had the option of going back to Ireland if he wanted, but he said, "I left my mother once; I cannot do it again." He loved his new country, had been willing to fight for it, and it now felt like home. He was awarded his U.S. citizenship shortly after returning from the war.

Grandpa and Grandma Morrow surprised their grandchildren with a pony when I was eight years old. Her name was Queen, and we called her Queenie. He liked to hitch her up to a newly painted bright red cart, and we drove her all around their farm. I loved that pony. I would ask to go brush Queenie and ride her as often as I could. I rode her bareback. She had a bad habit of bucking me off, but I didn't mind too much. My favorite thing was just to go see her and talk to her. I told her all my secrets, my eight-year-old troubles, how much I loved her, and what a good girl she was. I loved how she would always come up to me when I walked toward her gate.

Thoughts of Queenie and my grandparents faded slowly as we pulled into the driveway. Gary and I found out that we were all heading over to see a neighbor who had a pony they had hitched up to a cart. This neighbor was going to give us all a ride. I thought that was so cool, especially since I had just been reminiscing about Queenie and my grandparents.

We got to the neighbor's place, and I couldn't believe my eyes. There was Queenie! This pony looked exactly like Queenie. I was so excited to pet her, and I asked the neighbor what the pony's name was.

He said, "Queenie."

I dropped to the ground. Grief overcame me. The thoughts and visions I had had less than fifteen minutes before of my beloved maternal grandparents and pony, just a few months after my mom had died—well, it was all just too much for me to hold in.

I felt the presence of them all—Grandpa and Grandma Morrow, Queenie, and Mom—with me. Sobbing uncontrollably, I felt such love being sent to me from all of them circling around me. It was overwhelming in the most blessed way. After I had a chance to catch my breath, I shared this story with my granddaughter, Emma, who had kneeled next to me to be close to me, and we hugged tightly.

I will never forget that moment of clarity, all of those things coinciding at the perfect moment to bring me the love of my family and beloved pet from the Other Side that day. And with that Valentine's arrow of love piercing my heart, my grief began.

Some might call what happened with seeing the neighbor's pony, Queenie, a *coincidence*. As if these exact details of my thoughts about my beloved Queenie and my grandchildren's neighbor's horse had no connection. I believe it was connected. I believe it was a Divine sign to let me know my loved ones were thinking of me. I call this form of

Divine Intervention a Divine Pivotal Moment. Where something comes together that grabs your attention and your emotions. Where you really can't believe that it all happened and came together so perfectly. Where you find yourself asking, "What are the chances of that really happening?"

Have you experienced things like this in your own life?

How did you feel when it happened?

How did you explain it to yourself and others?

Close your eyes and ask what other examples you had in your life where you called something a *coincidence*. Write them down and focus on the details of how you felt when they were happening.

CHAPTER 11

Grief and Praying for a Medium

The pain of my loss had been in a holding pattern for five months as I focused my attention and energy on selling Mom's house, distributing her belongings, and handling estate closing details. Most of those details were completed by October. But with the emotional incident with my family and their neighbor's pony, Queenie, opening the floodgates, my grief engulfed me. I felt sad, forlorn, and inconsolable.

I attended our local hospice grief group. I sat and cried through the whole session. I was sitting in a group of seventy- and eighty-year-olds who had lost their spouses, and as I heard their pain, my heart sunk deeper. I couldn't even imagine losing my husband, especially after I had just lost my mom. The thought of that made me feel worse.

I even tried individual grief therapy for a couple of sessions, and while it was good, and I was grateful to receive it, I didn't feel like it was actually helping me feel better.

One day, I had a crazy idea. I thought, I am going to get an appointment with the Long Island Medium, get on a plane, and have a reading with Theresa Caputo. I had watched episodes of her TV show and saw how people were finding comfort with her readings.

I went online and felt defeated as I read that she was booked out for over two years. I felt so sad; I didn't feel like I could wait two years. A day or so later, I was watching another episode of her show, and she said that because she was booked out a long time into the future, she suggested that people turn to their local mediums. She said to ask friends for recommendations. I thought that was an excellent idea, but because I was so sad and exhausted, I had no energy to try and track down a medium.

So, like I had done so many times in my life, I started praying. I asked God to help me. I asked God to please help me find a medium if it would help me. I'd had other interesting Divine Intervention experiences in my life, and I'd had soul readings, but I'd never had a session with someone to talk with my deceased loved ones before. I wasn't sure how I felt about it, except that I knew my desperate desire for help outweighed my concern about whether it was the right thing to do. Besides, I had talked to God about it, and if He thought it was a good thing for me, then something would happen to connect me to a medium.

By this time, I felt depressed and was having trouble getting out of bed in the morning. I focused on completing my work appointments and spent time with my grandchildren, but I had no energy or enthusiasm for much else. One day, I needed some ink for my copier, so Gary talked me into going over to Staples with him. He thought it would be good for me to get out and about. I agreed. As I was leaving Staples, a friend I hadn't seen in a while, Deblyn Russell, was coming in. Deblyn is another great Light Worker who does massage and other forms of Divine Energy work. We visited a bit, and I told her about my mom's death.

Deblyn was hosting a Love and Light Circle at her church and invited me to come. I knew I wouldn't feel like going, but I appreciated being asked, and wrote the date and time on my calendar. The day of the event, I wasn't planning on going and tried to stay in bed. But what felt like a gentle but firm force was pushing me out of bed.

I thought this was so strange. I didn't really want to go, yet felt my body being moved to go through the motions of taking a shower, washing my face, getting dressed, and driving over to the church.

When I arrived, there were about 40 people in the room, all in a big circle. I tried to focus on what was happening and did feel peaceful. I enjoyed it. It had been months since I had felt that kind of peace. I was so grateful to God for bringing Deblyn and me together and for her kind invitation.

There was a woman sitting seven seats away from me, and I noticed I kept looking over at her. She looked back at me and smiled.

At the end of the service, I felt compelled to go over and talk to her. I told her this, and she said she felt like we were supposed to talk, too. We introduced ourselves to each other. She asked me what I did, and I said, "I'm a business and life mastery coach. What do you do?"

She said, "I'm a medium."

I let out a relieved and grateful sigh, looked up to God, and thanked Him silently.

I also felt appreciation for Deblyn's kindness and her part in the synergy of helping me find a medium. Gary was also instrumental, because this wouldn't have happened if he didn't make the initial suggestion that I go to Staples with him. I marveled at all the Divine forces and people at play in assisting me in finding this medium. We're all a part of a bigger Divine picture that we aren't always aware of. Miracles—big and small—happen around us, for us and others, every day. Being reminded of this can bring us peace and joy and allow our lives to unfold while we breathe easy, trusting in our Divine partnership to love, guide, and protect us.

This experience taught me that we are loved and cared for so much by God; He knows our situation and is working on everything for us behind the scenes. Praying is something I do every day. Not just at certain times, but throughout my day. I almost always have a running dialogue going on with God. Most of the time I'm saying, "Help! and Thank you!" I used to feel bad asking for so much, but I've learned that it's exactly what we are supposed to do. Ask so that we can receive.

The other thing is I trust God to deliver what I need. Not always what I want or how I want it, but what I truly need. When what I'm doing isn't working and I feel powerless, I try to remember to surrender it all to Him. And, honestly, it always turns out better for me in the long run. So much of the time, I am in a state of awe, as I couldn't have planned for things to work out any better than they do.

We must also surrender to the time frame. Sometimes that's difficult to do, but that's where the trust and faith come in. I trust that in His perfect time and His perfect way, I will be served in a way that's for the Highest Benefit of All. And when I get impatient? That's when I check in with my intuition. If I feel I am supposed to do something and act, I do. If not, I ask for patience and hang on. This chapter is a good example of hanging on and trusting that when the time was right, I'd receive what I'd asked for. And then when I got a literal nudge—one that pushed me out of bed—I followed through.

I confess, I used to be a worrywart. I would stress silently, or sometimes not so silently, especially when things weren't turning out the way I thought they were supposed to. But I have learned, often the hard way, that all that stressing is usually not helpful or healthy for myself or anyone else. When I forget and think I'm in control of everything, that usually turns out to be a huge mistake. I'm a planner, so I'm still working on all of this, just like anyone else. But I am getting better and better with time. I am making progress. We're all works in progress, and I've learned to be a lot more compassionate with myself over the years.

What are some of your favorite experiences from times when you were out of ideas, where you'd hit a major roadblock and decided to give it up to your Higher Power?

When you did, did things work out so much better than you had thought they would? Write down these memories. Let yourself breathe them in and find the peace that passes all understanding. That is your gift and mine.

CHAPTER 12

Carol's First Reading

On December 27th, 2012, I was fifty-five years old, and I had my first reading from a medium, Carol Mauer. My mom had died on May 22, 2012, a little over seven months before, and with my grief finally cracked open, I was hanging by a thread, overwhelmed by sadness.

I had met Carol several weeks before, as I mentioned, at Deblyn Russell's Christmas Love and Light Service, by nothing short of a finely woven miracle. After some desperate desiring and praying on my part, she appeared in that beautiful Christmas setting as if she'd floated down from the sky like Mary Poppins, wrapped in a big red bow. She even had the demeanor of Mary Poppins—competent, joyous, with light-filled, yet industrious intentions.

When we met, I shared with her that I would be leaving for Florida shortly after Christmas, and I wanted to fit in a reading before I left. She assured me that we could, and we scheduled it on the spot. I felt at ease with her immediately, and she shared with me that her own mother had passed literally within days of my own.

I noticed that she seemed to be doing better with her mother's death than I was. There was an ease and lightness about her, and I felt in awe of her abilities. I felt a desire to have that same ease and lightness in myself. Hmm. Maybe channeling the messages of our deceased loved ones revealed an ease and peace of understanding about death and dying that I had not discovered yet.

The morning of our appointment, as I prepared for her arrival, I brushed my hair and was looking at myself in the mirror when I exclaimed, "Maybe my great-grandmother Maggie will show up!" I'd heard so many wonderful stories about her from my mom that I felt it would be the cat's meow if she made an appearance. I tried not to have any expectations, but I had been thinking about this day ever since we'd set up the appointment. This was going to be the best Christmas present to myself I'd ever received, and I was excited.

The practical side of me, however, was a bit skeptical. I'd decided that I would require three accurate pieces of information from Carol before I would respond to anything she said. I know that sounds rather unfair. But to be clear and fair to Carol, I told her I was going to be a bit of a hard grader, because I knew people who might be interested in her services, and I wanted to be able to give a clear and unbiased recommendation. Even though I set a requirement for accuracy, I was very open to her doing the reading. And, as it turned out, she wasn't bothered by my requirements at all.

She arrived right on time, and as we walked into our living room, the loudest sounding train I had ever heard went by. Gary and I had lived in our home for nine years at the time. Mostly, the trains had become like white noise to us, and we barely noticed them chugging by. But not that day. I even said as we sat down, "I can't believe how loud that train is today! I usually never even notice them going by." She said nothing. Just smiled in a knowing way.

We got settled. I had my notebook and a pen on my lap, my water and a Kleenex box sitting on the side table next to me. I was ready.

Carol closed her eyes, then took a deep breath. The first thing she said was, "Your Mom is showing me what looks like something about accounting. She's showing me what looks like a checkbook. She's balancing a checkbook."

I froze for an instant but kept writing down everything Carol was saying, saying nothing in response. But I thought, my mom worked in a bank for thirty years. She helped hundreds of customers with their checking and savings accounts, but one of her superpowers was helping the bank balance its accounts to the penny, every day, without a computer. I wrote down the number "1" next to my note.

Then she said, "Your Mom is playing a piano. Now she's playing an organ. She's moving back and forth from the piano to the organ, and she's now singing as she's playing." Carol was laughing and told me, "Your mom is quite the gal. I'm enjoying her so much!"

I don't know what my face looked like. I was trying to stay blank. But I know I was breathing differently, and I felt on high alert. Again, I wrote all of this down, and I was thinking, "Oh, my God! My mom started learning how to play the piano when she was six or seven. She got really good by her high school years and played for all the music and chorus events. After she had raised her children, she began playing for church, and in her later years, played for every wedding, funeral, church event, sang in the choir, and gave piano lessons for almost thirty years to so many children in the county. Much of my mom's life was literally hopping from one piano to another piano or organ and singing through it all."

I wrote down the number "2" by this next section of my notes. I know. I know. I probably should have given her three points for this, but remember, I was being a hard grader.

Carol continued, "And remember that noisy train when I first got here? I didn't want to say anything then, but your mom came in on that train. She was riding on the front of that train!"

Okay, that was it. I wrote the number "3" down by what I had just transcribed from her words. And I couldn't contain myself any longer. In fact, that was when I started sobbing. I grabbed a Kleenex and covered my face as I shook my head back and forth.

"My mom loved going everywhere on a train!" I blubbered. "She's been to Chicago on the train several times, out to Colorado and California to see relatives, and out to Arizona to visit friends. My mom loved traveling, and her favorite way was by train."

I then excitedly filled her in on how she'd gotten all the other information correct about my mom. I needed to catch my breath, so I took a long drink of my water.

Carol continued. She asked me about having vertigo. I shared that I had had it bad when Mom moved to the nursing home and several years earlier when I changed careers from financial advising to coaching. She said that was all from the magnitude and speed with which I was growing spiritually and from all the evolving I was doing. She said that things happen very fast for me with my energetic spiritual transformations.

She told me how my mom's style of communicating was soft and direct and that mine was more direct, and it served me well. This was true about my mom and felt true about me. I had been a rather quiet child, but my careers in teaching, financial advising, and business and life mastery coaching had required me to show my confidence, not hold back, respect people's time, and tell people directly what they needed to hear.

Then Carol said, "Your mom is making pancakes. No, she's making waffles. She is putting waffles on five plates, one on each plate."

I started crying again. I loved my mom's homemade waffles. She made them almost every Sunday night. Something easy and quick. "Dang, I miss her waffles. They were so good! They were my favorite," I shared. "I have her recipe, but rarely make them. And there were five kids in my family."

Then Carol said, "A huge protector spirit is here."

I said, "Is it my dad?" It just felt like my dad was in the room.

She said, "Yes. And he's saying to remember the gift of visioning that you have. To not only look into other people's eyes to see their next steps, but to look in the mirror, into your own eyes, to see your own next steps."

Carol was moving on. I was writing as fast as I could while still keeping it legible, sniffling the entire time. She explained that she doesn't get names very often, but she was clearly getting one now. "I'm hearing Margaret. A Margaret is here. No, it's Maggie."

There it was. My beloved great-grandmother Maggie had decided to add her presence and make this reading not only the best Christmas gift I ever received but maybe the best gift of all time. I grabbed another Kleenex in half disbelief. I thought, how could this get any better? And then, it did!

My great-grandmother brought the whole clan with all their finery. She was holding a candy dish with beautiful chocolates. Her three daughters, my two great aunts and my beloved maternal grandmother Emily, came with their beautiful handiwork.

Carol said, "They're showing me doilies, embroidered pillowcases, lace-edged table runners."

I could hardly take it. I felt so emotional. My grandmother Emily, her two sisters, Mary and Margaret, and her mother, my great-grandmother Maggie, were known for their beautiful and perfect tatting, embroidery, and cross-stitching. Grandma Emily taught me how to tat when I was in junior high. They all were also known for being the best cooks and bakers. Not only did everything they touched taste delicious, but everything looked perfect and beautifully made.

Carol said, "You get your own love of excellence and mastery from your Great-grandmother Maggie!"

I could hardly breathe. I was doing my best to take it all in, but I felt that I wanted to ask a question about my family and find out if Mom had been okay with her funeral and the other decisions I'd made after her death.

Carol said, "Your mother is letting me know that she was pleased with all the decisions that were made and that there is no reason to worry about anything. She then shows me the waffles on the five plates again."

Carol continued, "Your mom is telling me that she and your dad gave each of you kids a foundation for life and that the waffle on your plate represents that. And each of their children can eat that waffle any way they want. You don't have to worry about your family members and how they are eating their waffles, nor do they need to be concerned with how you are eating your waffle. No one needs to be looking back on their life. Just go out and live your life the way you want to. It's your waffle! Eat it the way you want to."

Then Carol added, "Both of your parents are jumping up and down and pointing to the beautiful painting of the Angel in the light behind you. They are saying, "Just look forward to the light and don't look back. Just move forward."

By the time she was done, even Gary's Uncle Paul Fober had visited and encouraged me to continue my love of painting, art, and travel. In a single hour, I had been gifted with such wisdom and beautiful messages from Mom, Dad, Grandma Emily Morrow, two great-aunts, and my great-grandmother Maggie. I was so overcome and touched by their love and presence.

Carol remarked, "I have done so many readings, and I've never had this many loved ones show up before."

I said, "I know why they all came. They know how sad I have been and how much I have been suffering. They wanted to come and show me that I was not alone, that their love would always be with me, and that they were always nearby, whenever I needed them."

Carol agreed. "That's exactly right."

I will always remember that day, that reading, and how it opened me up more to this level of Divine Intervention. By being open, any thoughts of negativity or fear could not be present, and I received messages from my dear loved ones who came forward to love me and help me heal.

What are your thoughts and experiences about this form of Divine Intervention? Is it something you are open to?

I never thought about hiring a medium before my mother died, but when she did, I was in a place of deep pain. This pain caused me to open myself to communicating spiritually with her through a medium, and I will always be most grateful for that.

CHAPTER 13

Carol's Second Reading

The medium session that I had with Carol in December of 2012, a few months after my mom's passing, changed my life. I felt like it brought my connection to my parents' spirits to a place that I could understand better. I now knew that they, and my other deceased loved ones, were close by, available to me whenever I wanted them, whether I was thinking about them or not. It healed some of the despair and depression I had been feeling.

In many ways, I feel it saved my life.

Before the session I was in such deep despair that unless I had a work or family commitment, I didn't feel like getting out of bed. I felt myself spiraling down and had little interest in things that I usually enjoyed doing.

I felt like I had one foot on earth and the other foot wanting to be in Heaven. I had no intention of hurting or killing myself. I just wanted to be with my mother, and she wasn't here anymore.

It was interesting. When I shared this piece of my journey with others, the reactions I got varied. Those who had never experienced a loved one dying looked alarmed. Those who had gone through the pain and loss of a dear loved one's passing knew how I felt.

You can have some idea what it might be like, but until you've experienced it, you don't really know. I also think the closeness of the relationship makes a difference. I'm not saying that my mom and I agreed on everything. Our relationship, like most mother/daughter relationships, had some difficult times here and there. But I loved her very much, and I felt her love for me every day of my life.

When that changed with her death, I felt lost without it. Something that I had relied on for fifty-four years seemed suddenly gone. The pain of this loss dropped me to my knees. I felt it to the core of my being.

During my medium reading, I experienced my mom and other deceased loved ones in their spirit form. Once again, I felt that indescribable love that I thought was gone forever.

It lifted me up. Before my medium session with Carol, I didn't know how I could keep on living. After the session, I was able to keep both feet on the earth and knew that I could continue with this life.

I was able to turn the corner and start focusing on other parts of my life, even though I missed Mom terribly and would have huge waves of sadness throughout the days and months ahead.

One other gift that I received from Carol was a confirmation of something I had been sensing and experiencing in our home. We have two lights in the living room that had been blinking, it seemed, every time I walked into the room when the lights were on since my mom had died.

At first, I didn't think anything about it. Then my husband noticed it, too. I felt like it was Mom letting me know that she was there and watching. Even though we couldn't see her anymore, she was still there.

When I asked Carol about the flickering lights in the living room, she smiled and said, "Oh, yes, your deceased loved ones can do that." She confirmed that it was my mom and dad, both, doing it.

So now, not only do I have access to them and talk to them periodically through the day, but if I'm in our living room and the lights are on, we have quite a bit of fun. I'll say things to them like, "Aren't the grandkids a delight?" or "I miss you and feel your love." They always flicker back! Gary isn't quite so amused and doesn't really like the flickering, but when I turn the lights off in the evening before we go to bed, I say good night to them. The flickering lights are a wonderful experience of connection for me, and I always feel my parents' love whenever they flicker.

When I returned to Iowa from Florida in the spring of 2013, I wanted to connect with Carol Mauer again. She was about my age and had lost her mom close to when I had lost my mom. I enjoyed her so much that I wanted to get to know her better. So I invited her to meet me for lunch.

We enjoyed catching up, and about an hour into our conversation and meal, Carol asked, "Well, do you want to know who is here?"

I said, surprised, "Of course!"

She laughed and shared that my dad had been there the whole time, sitting next to me as my protector. He had his arm around my shoulders and patted my right shoulder like he was so proud of me.

And Mom was swirling around, too. "The banker wants to let you know that she's here."

Carol and I both laughed.

Then Carol said, "Your dad is giving me the name Michael."

I said, "I do have a friend named Michael. I was asked to help heal him quite some time ago, and he's doing well!"

Carol then said, "Your dad is telling you that you can do what you did for Michael for others, anytime. That you can facilitate in helping others heal themselves energetically, and he is reminding you of that."

Then Dad switched subjects. Carol said, "Your dad is saying the number eighteen, over and over."

At first, I drew a blank. Then I said, "Well, Gary and I have been married for eighteen years."

Then I said, excitedly, "Oh, he wants to acknowledge that he knows that the number eighteen is my favorite number. In the last five to eight years, eighteen has become an important number for me. The one means that we are all one, and the eight is the symbol of infinity and eternity. We are all one forever! Yes, it's my favorite number. He died before all of this. How did he know that?"

Carol grinned and looked at me like I should know by now how he knew that. I looked back at her with a delayed awareness and said, "Oh, yeah!"

Carol said, "There's a male spirit here now. He's telling me that you will know him because of his big red nose."

I thought for a second and said excitedly, "Oh, that's Stewart! One of my former clients. He was one of my favorites. We never talked about it, but he was like a father figure to me. He was always so kind and protective towards me. I miss him so much! Thank you so much for coming today."

The love I felt from my mom and dad, one of my favorite clients showing up for me, and their wonderful messages, was too much. I shook my head and pulled a Kleenex out of my purse.

I shared with Carol how overwhelmed and touched I felt. I thanked her and told her how amazing this was for me to experience. I cried with tears of love and joy.

Then she said, "You may not realize it fully yet, but you are just like me. You are a highly intuitive person."

As I gasped, I felt what she was saying was partly true. "Oh, is that what's been happening? I do feel like I have known things that others have not known my entire life. And while I have accepted it, I haven't really talked with anyone about it much. About what it all was."

I continued, "But, I'm not sure I can channel deceased loved ones. I sense them and sometimes see shadows, but I can't say I'm able to do what you are doing. Is it possible to expand my abilities, and if so, how would I do that?"

Carol answered, "Yes. Start meditating."

Do you meditate? If you do, how has it changed your life?

I came to find out in the months ahead how it would change my own life.

CHAPTER 14

Meditation and Time to Heal

When Carol Mauer shared with me that I was highly intuitive, just like her, I was stunned. I had never heard anyone talk about me in this way. I'd had other energetic readings before and had always been amazed by other people's gifts, but I had never included myself in this category of someone having supernatural gifts.

I had always felt a strong spiritual connection to God and Jesus and had claimed them as my primary relationships. That was not in question. And I had always felt like I knew things that a lot of people didn't seem to know. I just hadn't given it much thought. I accepted it, relied on it, felt grateful for it, but hadn't made a big deal of it. I was amazed when other people noticed it. Maybe by relying on it, I had also taken it for granted.

After talking with Carol and witnessing her incredible abilities as a medium, I was filled with wonder. Having this new piece of information about myself was thrilling, yet baffling.

It took me a while to digest it all. I thought and wondered about it—a lot. And I did cherish it. Having it acknowledged by someone else made it real to me. I felt very grateful and appreciative. Some days I felt lost, and I let it overwhelm me at times. It took a while to get used to the idea of being highly intuitive, but I did make one big change in my life after Carol and I said goodbye that day.

I started meditating.

While I never really considered it meditating, I knew how to relax and was always able to take a break and rest from any activity when I wanted to. I had a ritual of praying since I was a small child. And I always said prayers before sleep and before I got out of bed in the morning.

I decided that I would start meditating after my prayers both at night and in the morning. I also decided that I would try to go to bed a little earlier each night and wake up a little earlier, so I would have the extra time for meditation. I wasn't sure what to expect, but I absolutely loved meditating. I closed my eyes, totally relaxed, and felt like I could do it all day. It became one of my favorite times of the day. I started waking up earlier without my alarm, so I stopped setting it. Since the spring of 2013, I have been meditating for between fifteen minutes and two hours every day.

There are many books about meditation, with a lot of dos and don'ts. For me, I found that lying in bed before I go to sleep and after I wake up, before I get out of bed in the morning, works beautifully. Sometimes, I sit in a chair and meditate at various times during the day, but I like my morning and nighttime meditation rituals. It feels natural to me, and I don't have to figure out how to fit it in to another part of my day.

I also like to add healing and body rejuvenation prayers and affirmations to my meditation times. I will simply thank God for the gift of my body to heal itself perfectly. I ask that if there is anything that needs to be adjusted, that I trust this will be taken care of for me, and then I give thanks. Another favorite affirmation that I like to focus on while meditating is *Feel the Love*. This is when I focus on connecting to the powerful force of love that is our Creator/God. I do my best to do this daily, as it is always a powerful and amazing feeling of connection for me.

I encourage others to try different times, locations, and ways to meditate to figure out what works best for them. I find doing the dishes or preparing food rather therapeutic and meditative. Drying my hair, taking a walk, looking up at the sky, tending my flowers in the summer, even some forms of exercise are forms of meditation for me, too.

Meditation became a new and beloved ritual for me, and I looked forward to how my intuitive abilities might expand, as well. What I hadn't anticipated was that the dam that held back my emotions would break open.

I think trying to recover and process the pain of losing my mom also opened me up to healing and processing pain that had been inside of me since childhood. With meditation, I found myself relaxing more, and maybe that helped me feel safe enough to allow feelings to surface that I had kept down for years. I really don't know, but I was back to processing pain.

It was exhausting and frustrating, but I sensed this was what I needed to do. I had read about how others processed their pain and learned that I needed to give myself the time to feel my pain, cry, and let myself have the time to feel what I had pushed aside. I needed to tend to myself and my feelings.

I thought how genius that was. For most of my life, when I felt sad, scared, angry, hurt, or disappointed with situations or people, it never seemed like there was any time or opportunity to care for myself. So I just stuffed whatever was happening inside and moved on. I think that's what many of us do. Life moves fast. If you don't know how to tend yourself, and if, when you were a child, your caretakers either didn't know how to care for you emotionally or were at work or too busy, your feelings can get pushed to the side.

I read about a woman who had lost her child. She was understandably devastated and inconsolable. She stayed in bed for the better part of two years. I'm sure she got out of bed to eat and take care of the basics of her life, but she allowed herself to tend her feelings instead of forcing herself to swallow them and move on. This made so much sense to me, so I used this as a guide to process the pain from my own mom's passing.

I don't think our culture properly supports the processing of our grief and pain. With families having parents in demanding jobs, rearing children, following crazy schedules to fit in exercise, volunteering, and attending all their kids and grandkids sports and other activities, even when someone in our life dies or becomes ill, we plunge right back into our fast-moving lives. We take a few days off, maybe, but that's it.

I think grief has its own way with people. If we ignore it, I think it can set us up for poor health and suffering that only gets worse if we continue to run away from it. With my own business, which allows me to have a flexible schedule, and the fact that I was in my fifties when this all happened, it seemed to be the perfect recipe for: "You are going to process this now!"

Our bodies and minds are so fascinating. I looked at my schedule to see when I had appointments or time with grandchildren. I focused on what I needed to get done, but I also stopped adding clients for a while and stopped writing the business e-newsletter that I had written for eight years. Anything I didn't HAVE to do, I let go of.

I didn't say, "Okay, today I'm going to stay in bed and try to feel better." No, I felt bad, had no energy, and tried to get out of bed, but my body was not cooperating. It's as if my body knew my schedule. It would cooperate for the most part when I had commitments. When my schedule was free, my body let go. When I surrendered to it, I felt like a dead weight.

There were days when I had to force myself to get out of bed and eat. Sometimes, Gary would just bring me something easy to eat like an orange and an egg sandwich, and I ate it in bed. We figured it out and made life work. I told Gary up front that I didn't know how long I would feel like this. I wanted to be fair to him. I knew I wouldn't be able to be there for him during this time like I'd like to be. Thank God he understood and was there for me.

I'd cry and sob until the tears from that wave of pain were done. Then, because I was so exhausted, I'd sleep. I had no intention of getting prescription drugs. I am highly sensitive and knew that wouldn't be my path. I can't even take an aspirin without feeling out of sorts and overstimulated. I surrendered to the pain and prayed to God that I could get through it. I gave myself to it and hoped eventually I would come to the end of this dark tunnel I was in.

The days went by. After a period of sobbing, I would feel a little better and hope that I had turned the corner, only to be back in a wave of sadness the next day. I told myself day after day, "It's okay. You're getting it out. That session is over. You're making progress."

I gave up any attempt to exercise for a while. I'd think about it and then think I was out of my mind for even considering it. One day, after I'd been in this cycle for about eight months, I started feeling slightly better. It seemed as if the sobbing cycles had lessened. I had this crazy idea that I could get out of bed, put my exercise clothes on, and try to exercise.

I made it to my closet. Then my legs stopped working. I dropped to the carpet and was on all fours. I crawled to the sink to splash some water on my face. I raised myself up and looked in the mirror.

I've never been more frightened for myself than when I saw my face in the mirror in that moment. When I looked in the mirror, I saw my red, raw face muscles. It looked like I had been skinned alive.

Again, I dropped to my knees and cried out in horror. There was no one with me. Gary was in Canada fishing for a week. What was going on? I didn't know, but I crawled back to my bed and got in it. I shook until I fell asleep.

I don't know if I will ever know what happened to me that day. But whatever it was, it was as if I was being shown visually how I felt emotionally. It was as if all the pain and suffering I had tolerated and withstood in my life left me feeling like I'd been skinned alive.

I cried for myself that day. I still cry when I think about it. I'm crying right now as I write this. It was devastating. If this had happened to someone else, my heart would have broken for them. It was as if I needed to be shown what I didn't want to face. What I didn't want to know about me. What I didn't want to see.

This was another Divine turning point for me. I think that I was supposed to realize that my habit of pushing my hurt feelings away and moving ahead with life was not smart. Trying to speed ahead and hope I was done healing and forcing myself to feel better before I did feel better was not going to be in my best interest, either.

This turning point introduced me to having true compassion for myself. I realized I was good at giving others compassion but not so much for myself. It hit hard. I had to admit that I'd failed that test in life, and this was a wake-up call. Things started making more sense to me, and I began to look at some of my behaviors. I had always been a people pleaser, and I was finding that as I got older, it was literally wearing me out.

When my mom got sick, I was so glad I was able to be there for her. When she died, I was filled with sorrow and despair. With these heavy emotions I was feeling, along with the added stress and responsibilities of her illness and death, it was only a matter of time before I broke down.

It took me about two years of intermittent time in bed and healing before most of the pain dissipated. From the middle of 2013 to the middle of 2015, I was in bed one to two days every week, depending on my schedule. Many times, it would start with a severe pain in my back, feeling like a knife was cutting into me. Over time, it lessened to about one day every two weeks.

What a difference! I was so grateful and honestly felt I could see the light at the end of this tunnel. I gradually had a down day maybe once every three weeks, and it just kept getting less and less. I was feeling better and better, and I started enjoying and engaging in life again.

After I was pretty much back to normal, I started thinking about all that had happened and what I had experienced and learned.

After going through so many days of feeling terrible and experiencing pain I didn't want to feel, I could see that facing it and surrendering to it allowed me to get through it. I witnessed my own courage day after day as the emotional pain ebbed and flowed. Some days, I would pray that it would stop. Other days, I didn't have the energy to think. I just endured. I had compassion for Gary, too, as I watched him sit with me, unable to do anything to help me except witness my pain and look at me with sincere love and concern. He was helpless to help me, and I was helpless to make it stop. We both surrendered to it.

This was my Dark Night of the Soul. I needed to go through it to heal, and through facing my own pain, I gained a perspective about other people's suffering. I feel it prepared me for being there for other people as they suffered their own losses, hurts, demons, and disease. I don't know anyone who hasn't suffered at some point in their life, whether physically, mentally, emotionally, or all of them combined. Life can be full of bumps, bruises, and sorrows. I thought about specific people in my life and what their lives must be like as they journeyed through pain and suffering from disease, loss of loved ones, financial stresses, relationship breakups, and other struggles.

I realized that my relationship with God was my primary support. I could talk to Him whenever I wanted. And Gary brought me love, friendship, and companionship every day.

And I learned that I could be there for myself. That was a crucial point in my transformation. It was something I hadn't been able to do before.

I thought about what my life was like before the pain broke through. What would my life be like now? What parts of my before-life would change? What would I decide to let go of forever? What new pieces would I want to add to my life?

I'm still asking and answering these questions. But I can share a few of the changes I've made so far.

I don't take on so many things at once anymore. I have more compassion for myself and how much I can handle and do in a day. I still like to accomplish things, but I am very selective about what I choose to do. And I let myself change my mind if I need to. I prioritize better and let some things go. I give myself as much compassion as I give others. I don't have to do everything in one day. I can stop a project in midair if I need to. I take a lot more breaks, and I'm not such a hard grader, for myself or others.

I laugh at myself more and don't care if I make mistakes. Life is easier and less stressful. If I don't want to do something, I don't do it. I understand if others don't want to do things, so I hope they can understand if I don't, too. I still enjoy pleasing people, but I say no if it feels like too much. I consider myself in the mix of everything I do. I feel I'm more content and able to really be there for people. If I'm not able to be there, then I say no, and trust that others can fill in the gaps. I ask for help more often and don't feel like I must figure out everything by myself.

I also trust people to find their own solutions and figure things out for themselves without worrying about them. I trust myself more, too.

In some ways, I felt like my soul needed to go through all of this so I could fully understand the Dark Nights of other's lives, too. We all suffer. Can we be with others through their suffering? Can we be with ourselves through our own suffering? Until we can experience our own unbearable suffering, I'm not sure we can relate to and help others fully.

I am grateful to people who share the rough times in their lives so that we all can utilize and benefit from what worked for them—and so we don't feel so alone in our own suffering. That's another reason I decided to share some of the rough times in my own life. I know there are people who are suffering, and we can help and connect with each other. I didn't feel so alone after I learned how others healed their own pain. It opened possibilities of ways to heal that I resonated with when the right time to heal came for me.

And I have a secret weapon that really isn't a secret. I trust that my Divine Partnership with God lets me surrender everything when I have no idea how to solve situations or I get myself into a rut. I stay aware and awake to getting Divine signs and messages that make everything better. I rely on this Divine Partnership on a daily, even minute by minute basis. And I hope that the stories I share in this book will be as powerful for you and your own life as they have been for me. I hope they stimulate your thinking and your memories to awaken you to your own powerful Divine Partnership that will make all the difference in your life.

Have you had your own Dark Night of the Soul? How did you care for yourself? How did you get through it? What did you learn about yourself? What changes did you make in your life because of it? Give yourself time to think and journal about it and reflect on the perspectives you have about it now.

CHAPTER 15

Guardian Angel

During the spring of 2013, I had signed up to attend the Women's Spirituality Conference in Mankato, Minnesota, that would be taking place in October of that year. I had wanted to go for years, but my work schedule always got in the way. I sent in my registration so I would have something to look forward to after going through the sadness from my mom's death the year before. As the date approached, I worried that I wouldn't feel like going. This was during my depression and healing time, and I was relieved when my husband offered to drive and take me home early if it became too much.

On the day we left for the conference, I felt no sadness or depression. In fact, I was feeling the best I'd felt in a long time. I was encouraged to feel how excited and happy I was. My soul must have been so happy because I knew I would be surrounded by women who were there to celebrate women enjoying their spiritual connections.

I'd signed up for a breakout session with a woman named Maria Gurney Peth. Her workshop was about seeing auras, the colored energy around people, and we'd be practicing getting messages with a partner in the group. I was amazed when she introduced herself and shared where she was from. I had never met her before, but her office was in Waverly, only fifteen miles away from me.

I had heard about people seeing auras and thought it would be interesting. I was astonished by how clearly I could see yellows and soft oranges when I closed my eyes as Maria took us through several exercises. It was fun, but I enjoyed the exercise where we practiced getting messages with a partner even more.

When it was my turn to do the reading for my partner, I felt so indescribably good. It felt comfortable, enjoyable, and fun. I can't remember the details of what either one of us picked up, but I do remember the essence of what happened. My partner in the class was able to pick up some key things about my personality, and I was able to pick up on a wedding or some family event that she was involved with. We were only given a couple of minutes, but I was amazed how connected I felt with this woman.

Maria was also giving mini-readings in the large vendor area, so I signed up for one. I was very curious about what she would tell me. It was quite loud in this setting, as there were probably over fifty vendors in this large area. I had scheduled my time so that I could walk through and check out the vendors who interested me before my mini-reading. There were many women giving Divine Energy readings; vendors with beautiful crystals, each with their own specific healing properties; flowing, colorful clothing; books; sound bowls being played; CDs of music for meditating; pendulums; and many other items that intrigued me. I could have spent a week there, as I was fascinated with almost everything I saw and heard.

I was surrounded by beautiful women of all ages and backgrounds. I felt a longing to stay and spend more time with every person I met. They all had generous and uplifting energies—both the attendees and the vendors. I loved every minute I spent there.

I was exhilarated by the time I sat down with Maria for my reading. She closed her eyes and told me, "You are a teacher, a spiritual teacher. You will be doing more of your work in the future when you understand this."

I was taking notes, and she continued, "You also have many spiritual, intuitive gifts, like me, and more are emerging."

This was the second confirmation of my abilities. I'd received very similar information from two different mediums within six months. First Carol Mauer and now Maria.

I was grateful for this reading and pondered in my open heart what would happen as my life unfolded.

One day shortly after the Women's Spirituality Conference, I was reading in my office when I suddenly remembered something Maria had said in her workshop. She said that we all have at least one Guardian Angel. While they don't care if we call them by their names, they do have names, and we can ask them what it is.

I laid on my office sofa thinking about this for a while. I thought, "Why not ask?" So, I did.

Suddenly, I was shown and could see clearly the name FLORENCE in big, block-like, black and tan letters. They were floating straight across the room, about ten inches in front of my face. I also got the feeling that these letters had been stamped on my forehead at the same time with a big black stamp. And whatever spiritual entity had done the stamping was in a hurry, was busy, but was going to answer my question, and they wanted me to remember their answer.

As soon as I was given this name, I thought, "Florence Nightingale." At first, I thought I was being given the name Florence Nightingale to help me remember the name Florence. But then I started wondering about who Florence Nightingale was. I knew she had been a nurse, as I had read about her when I was in grade school. I felt I was being given confirmation that this was true. I quickly Googled her name. I learned that she believed nursing was her Divine purpose. She served the British Army in the Crimean War in 1854. She was known for being concerned with sanitation and its relation to mortality. She worked endlessly, caring for the wounded soldiers, and was called "The Lady with the Lamp." The London Times referred to her as a "ministering Angel." Her work in the field brought public health to national attention. She was one of the first people in Europe to grasp the principles of the new science of statistics and apply them to military and later civilian hospitals. In 1907, she was the first woman to be awarded the Order of Merit. She was especially remarkable for her intelligence, determination, and amazing capacity for work.

In a recent conversation with Maria Gurney Peth, she shared with me that our Guardian Angels are part of God's Right Hand and have not lived on earth. Maybe some of the essence and qualities of Florence Nightingale would not only help me remember Florence's name but provide some insight into the amazing capabilities that my Guardian Angel had. And I thanked God for putting my care in such good hands.

And, speaking of good hands, since my thirties, I have been interested in what I'd heard and read about the benefits of different natural healing modalities, such as massage, Reiki, reflexology, and many others. I started having massages regularly in my thirties and have had some wonderful Reiki healing sessions that always left me feeling fabulous. I've always felt I had excellent health, but had experienced tight muscles sometimes, and I'm a huge proponent of massages to stay energetically balanced.

I was referred to Kate Thoma, a local massage therapist, over thirty years ago by a friend. I started out with a monthly massage. It was such a wonderful healing and relaxing experience; I quickly went to twice a month massages. From my life coaching classes through Coach U, I learned about the practice of extreme self-care and soon was on a weekly massage schedule. I loved this experience so much that I secretly thought about what it would be like to have a daily massage.

Kate also has the gift of reading soul energy. After every massage, I was treated to her Divine messages of guidance and support.

With reflexology, the idea that all the major organs and body systems were connected in the foot fascinated me, and I asked the Divine Energy System to help me find a reflexologist.

A few weeks later, I was driving by some stores and noticed what seemed like a new Reiki business that had a big sign saying they were having an open house the next day. "Huh," I thought, "I wonder if they have anyone in there that does reflexology?"

So I parked my car and went in. I was told they had invited a local reflexologist for the open house, and I made an appointment through the owner for a session that next day. (No surprise, right? I'm amazed how fast our Angelic Guides and Divine Energy System figure out how to guide us to the right place in such quick order.)

When I walked in for my appointment, I met Sandra "Sandy" Praska and immediately felt comfortable and hopped up on her massage table. It felt so good! Sandy was very skilled; she had the right amount of pressure that woke me up and then felt good by the time the pressure was released. While she was expertly massaging and tweaking pressure points around different areas of my feet, she and I behaved like long lost friends making up for the time we'd missed away from each other. We gabbed and laughed through the whole hour session. I felt like not only had God and His Divine Energy System found me an expert reflexologist but also a wonderful new friend. She was also trained as a Reiki practitioner and in several other alternative healing modalities. I still rely on her expert training and gifts for myself and recommend her to others, as well.

I realized that I had been highly interested in meeting and experiencing the benefits from many different natural healing practitioners over the years, while simultaneously collecting them as wonderful friends and resources for others. I felt a kinship with them. Like they were all working together and serving others for their highest good. And in a natural and holistic way. They are my Light Worker and Soul Sister community, and I have been blessed beyond measure with their presence in my life.

How do you take care of yourself?

Have you resonated with any forms of alternative and body work healing modalities and/or the professionals who administer them?

What are your favorites? I encourage you to pay attention to what types of self-care you resonate with and treat yourself whenever possible.

CHAPTER 16

I Love You, I Love You!

In March of 2014, while in Florida, I was awakened in the middle of the night. I heard the Voice that I'd heard many times before, that I now referred to as the voice of the Holy Spirit, or Spirit.

It said to me, "*Say, I love you.*"

I immediately said, "I love you."

I felt such love from this Divine Presence that I started weeping.

This was a different type of crying from the crying and sobbing during my emotional healing that I had been doing for almost a year by then. This felt like a Divine communication of love was being sent to me to let me know that God and Jesus, through the Holy Spirit, were with me. That I was being tended by God, as well as by myself. That I was loved, watched over, and not alone.

I took a breath and blew my nose.

I heard, "*Say it again. Say, I love you.*"

I said it again, "I love you."

I heard, "*Say it again. Over and over.*"

I whispered it over and over, probably twenty times, "I love you. I love you. I love you."

I felt myself shifting. I felt myself opening to a new and higher level of love. But what kind of love?

In the first moments, I felt God's love for me. Then, the shift felt like it was also about self-love, something being taught to me that I needed to improve on. Like a piece of self-evolution that I needed as I moved forward with my life in this world.

As I continued saying it over and over, it felt like I was downloading a love for myself; it was a new and different feeling. I felt like it would protect me from others who might have rejected me in the past. I had a feeling that I would not feel dejected by my encounters with others who I sensed didn't agree with me. In the past, I would feel lost from this sense of rejection; now I would have understanding and acceptance, both for myself and others, in a way that I couldn't quite get to before.

I don't know how long this Divine interaction lasted, maybe a half hour.

I fell asleep again and, in the morning, shared what I'd experienced with Gary. He was as amazed as I was.

I felt the same, but different, too. It felt like I had a new and better perspective, and I was full of gratitude.

A month after my early morning "I love you" interaction with Spirit, we flew to Maui for two weeks. One evening, Gary and I were finishing a lovely dinner outside, watching the waves smash onto the shore. We decided to go listen to some live music that we could hear happening a short walk away. The music turned out to be a one-man band, and he was fantastic. When he took breaks, he visited with people at their tables. We had such a great time talking, and he was so interesting. I asked him if he had ever written any of his own songs, and he replied that he hadn't. I told him I'd always wanted to write songs with other people. We joked a bit about that, and I said that if he wasn't doing anything tomorrow afternoon, maybe we could meet and write a song together. We laughed, even though I really wished it could happen.

Early the next morning, around 5:00 a.m., I was awakened. A song was coming. I could hear it. It was a song about the "I love you" experience I'd had back in Florida.

I got out of bed because both the music and the lyrics were coming through. I couldn't believe it! I thought I better hurry up and find some paper to write it down before I forgot it. It came fast and clear. And this is what I was given and wrote down:

The I Love you, I Love You Song
by God and Karoleen Fober, written 4-22-14

And God said I love you, now repeat after Me,
    I love you; I love you, He said tenderly.
    I love you; I love you. Again, and again.
    I love you; I love you. I love you, Amen!

Now morning and evening, throughout your day,
    Just say it; just say it. It is the way.
    I love you; I love you. Again, and again.
    I love you; I love you. I love you, Amen!

Stand up and sing/say it. Again, and again.
Share how it's working, in your/my life, Amen!
    I love you; I love you. Again, and again.
    I love you; I love you. I love you, Amen!

While I was half-wishing the day before that I could write a song with the singer who had serenaded us, I guess God had a different plan for the song and the way and time it would be delivered. Maybe He was reminding me that He is my Chief Co-Creator and encouraging me to rely on Him even more. People are busy, have their own commitments, schedules, and desires. I had my own ideas and wishes about how the song would arrive, but God delivered it in the perfect time and way. It's a very simple, yet powerful song. I feel like it's also a poem and affirmation. I sing it softly, almost like a lullaby or a love song.

God told me it was a song of healing, transformation, and a reminder of how to live in the physical world but with your Spiritual Lifeline and Communication intact. I believe we are all children of God, and we are bits of the Highest Love that we came from and will eventually return to. We are never alone. We are so loved. We are meant to co-create with our Source. All in God's time and way.

What magical experiences have you had where a thrilling insight or a breakthrough solution or song has come through for you?

Were you able to capture it and experience the gift fully?

How did it affect you or change you and your life?

I encourage you to give yourself time to sit with these questions and write down what emerges. Remember to date your responses, as it will give you a rich perspective of your own Divine Intervention moments timeline.

CHAPTER 17

Love from My Grandmothers

In March of 2015, I was feeling much better, and my sad days were fleeting. I thought about all my Divine Intervention experiences. I felt so grateful for everything that had happened and for all the wonderful people who had served me at such a difficult time in my life.

I decided to call Carol Mauer and a few other people who had helped me and offer them a complimentary soul reading. I felt my own ability to read the Divine Energy of other's souls was opening and expanding. I wanted to serve others and decided to start with people I knew.

I also thought of my grandmothers and all the wonderful times we'd had together and how much I missed them. I shared some of my favorite stories about them with Gary, and we laughed and laughed. I asked Gary if he thought my grandparents could see us and our grandchildren and if they knew how much I loved and missed them. He said he wasn't sure but thought they did. After my reading with Carol, I believed the same thing.

It was so much fun talking with Carol on the phone. She decided to wait until I returned to Iowa for her reading, so we could see each other, too. I was fine with that but had made the decision that I was able to do readings on the phone. I had coaching clients all over the United States, and I loved the ease of serving these people by phone. I had used my intuitive abilities with my clients for years, not really knowing how to describe what was happening. I was just picking up on their energy and the Divine Energy System's frequencies and sharing what I was getting.

After we finished catching up, Carol told me there were two female energies that she was picking up on and she wanted to know if I wanted their messages. I emphatically said, "YES!!!"

Carol reported the first female energy was showing her a huge basket of beautiful flowers. All kinds of flowers. Roses, petunias, daisies, and they were all beautiful colors with reds, pinks, yellows, and purples. She said they were gorgeous. Behind this woman, she saw flower gardens everywhere.

I said, "That must be my maternal grandmother, Grandma Morrow. She grew the most beautiful flowers and had gardens everywhere. She grew literally hundreds of flowers. She won ribbons for her flowers and flower arrangements at the county fair every year."

Then Carol said, "The other female energy is showing me a large book that she's holding. She's showing me that her hair is in a bun."

"Hmm, I can't think of who that would be," I said.

Carol added more information, "She is showing me her hands, and they are crippled, and her fingers are bent together like she had arthritis."

"Oh, that would be my paternal grandmother, Grandma Harryman. Yes, she had bad arthritis in her hands and feet. And she never cut her hair. She would braid it and wrap her long braid around and around into a bun. I loved watching her do this every morning when I stayed with her as a child. The book is a Bible. If she wasn't fixing meals or helping Grandpa, she was sitting with her Bible, reading it to herself or others," I shared.

"Now the other grandmother is showing me these glass globe-like containers that have water in them that are lit up. They are all on a Christmas tree," Carol described.

"Oh, those were her beautiful, old-fashioned Christmas lights that I loved so much. I could sit for hours just looking at how beautiful her tree always looked every Christmas," I exclaimed. I closed my eyes and visualized this memory.

I shared with Carol how Gary and I were just talking about both of my grandmothers the last couple of days. I was amazed that they came through and shared those things with Carol.

She said, "Whenever you think or talk about your loved ones, they hear you and know what's going on with your life."

"So when I feel their presence, they're really there?" I asked.

And Carol said, "Yes, absolutely!"

This information was so reassuring to me. It brought me comfort and helped me not be so scared of my loved ones dying. Yes, it would be different. Maybe I wouldn't be able to see them or hear them. But I could know that their spirits were present and always accessible. I could talk with them and tell them things. I could ask them questions and sense their answers.

When my Grandma Morrow died, I was nineteen years old. I was devastated and took it hard. She had lived a good life and was eighty-four when she passed. I felt so close to her. I had planned to read a story I had written about her when I was in my high school creative writing class for the funeral, but I was so emotional, I just couldn't do it.

What I noticed back then is that even though she had died, I felt like she was with me all the time. And I did talk with her and think about her all the time. So, maybe because I had never really talked about it with anyone, I didn't realize that what I was experiencing, the feeling of closeness with her, was really happening.

Because I was in college and away from home before she died, I didn't see her or talk to her that much. Cell phones hadn't been invented in 1976, and because you were charged extra, long-distance calls were made sparingly. After her death, because I could feel and sense her close by, I felt like she was in my life more than she had been when she was alive, and I thought about her more, too.

I was relieved I was beginning to add this understanding and perspective to my life. It made life easier knowing that when my loved ones died, it would be a different experience, but there would still be communications with them, just not in the way it had been when they were living in their bodies in the physical world.

Do you experience your loved ones who have left the physical world? If so, how do you describe these experiences?

Part III

Never the Same Again—My Divine Gifts Expand

CHAPTER 18

The BIG Question

It was the summer of 2015; I was feeling much better, pretty much felt back to my old self. Except that I had been changed by my mother's death, which had happened three years earlier.

I felt like I had a stronger understanding of death and knew how to accept it a little more easily. The fact that I had been able to find a medium who could contact my mom, who had proved to me that this connection was real by her accuracy in knowing things about my mother, gave me a new lease on life—and death.

It wasn't just that she knew and shared things about my mother. It was more than that. It felt like she and my mother were having a very important conversation with the whole goal of helping me with my sadness, grief, and questions, so that I could find peace and move on with my own life and missions. It felt like an act of lifesaving. I had been treading water in a deep ocean of despair, becoming more exhausted and hopeless by the day. Meeting with the medium was a life preserver that brought me back to shore.

I don't think I will ever be able to say that death doesn't affect me, but my recent experiences had started to give me a sense of peace and some relief about the subject. My old dread and resistance to the idea of my loved ones dying began to shift as I developed the awareness that I could still communicate with those who had crossed over. And they weren't gone—they had transformed.

The gift I had been given felt Divine and miraculous. I was in awe of Carol's ability to do what she did with such ease, love, and joy. And I spent time marveling about it and wondering how she did it.

I was in bed one night, meditating and feeling like I could probably fall asleep soon. The Voice speaking to me caught me by surprise when it said, *"Do you want to see and communicate with deceased loved ones?"*

I shot to high alert and froze!

The first thoughts that jumped into my head were that I might be frightened to see and speak to them, and if I were going to be scared all the time, I didn't want to do it. So, I spoke silently, "NO!" and shook my head back and forth emphatically.

I waited for more. But that was all the Holy Spirit had to say to me that night. It left me on my own to wonder about this question that I had just been asked.

Over the next couple of months, it was on my mind constantly. I was having a running conversation with myself about it. The first couple of weeks were all about me being scared. And I felt like I didn't know anything about how to do it, that I should know what I was doing, and if I didn't know what I was doing, then I had to say no. That made total sense to me. Good. End of subject.

But that wasn't the end of the subject. I started thinking about how I was able to use my intuition easily and without effort. I didn't really learn how to do it; I just did it. Maybe my focus was somehow different in those moments, but I didn't think so. When I was a kid, it just happened. When I was coaching my clients, it just happened. A good idea or a piece of information just appeared, like a perfect gift, even though I wasn't clear where it was coming from. I was always amazed and grateful, sometimes perplexed, but over time had come to accept that this was how I was—how God made me. I'd been like this for as long as I could remember.

And my intuition was a good thing. A really good thing. The pieces of information that popped in were always helpful, at least in the long run. It might take me a little while to understand what they were about, but they always contained helpful information.

I started adding a few things up. Hmm. Sometimes clear and helpful immediately. Always clear and helpful in the longer term. Always important, usually good, and if it was bad, it turned out to be for protection. And using my intuition was relatively easy.

When I watched Carol give me the reading, she didn't look like she was struggling, suffering, or afraid. She was perfectly composed, just sitting there with a perfect ease, looking comfortable and responding to me and my deceased loved ones like she was enjoying it.

My fear around receiving the gift of mediumship began to dissipate. I started thinking about how thankful I had been to receive my readings and how much they had helped me. I am positive it helped save me from going to a darker place and feel it saved my life, or at least helped me turn the corner from the dark place I was in. I was stuck in a big way back then, and Carol's mediumship and my loved ones' messages helped me get unstuck.

I also thought that if God thought I could utilize this gift for the benefit of others, then I should really accept the challenge. Why would He ask if He didn't think I could do it?

I kept going. I thought, I know how much I was suffering after my mom's death. If I said yes, then I could possibly try to help others through their loss and suffering. That was what did it. The thought of others suffering like I had made me so sad and heartbroken, exactly the state I had been in before, but now I had the chance to do what Carol did for me for others. I had the chance to step up and help others as I had been helped, in this very special way. It was now time, God willing, for me to try and help others who also might be hurting.

So, that very night, with this new perspective and conviction, I said, "Yes." I added, "God, if you feel I am worthy of this Divine gift, then I say yes to receiving it and helping your people for the Highest Benefit of All."

Do you feel you are being called to serve in new and different ways?

Do you feel your own Divine gifts expanding and strengthening?

Consider journaling about these questions and notice what is emerging in your life.

CHAPTER 19

Four Mediums and Self-Readings

In the summer of 2015, another important event happened that helped me with my emerging mediumship. I attended a Divine Energy Group Reading that Carol Mauer, along with three other local mediums, Bonnie Winninger, Dee Loecher, and Laurie Hazel, also friends of hers, were having. It was in Carol's home, and there were probably ten other women attending, including myself. We sat in a circle in the living room, and the four mediums took turns sharing the Divine information they were being given, doing a mini-reading with each person.

I didn't know any of the other people at the group reading, so I watched closely to see how people were reacting. Everyone seemed to be enjoying themselves, taking in the information. A couple of people did ask questions, and the mediums responded with brief answers. I thought it was a good way to let people have a mini-experience, and I couldn't wait for my reading.

When it was my turn to receive information, I was ready to take notes. Laurie said, "The Angels want you to keep journaling and writing."

Bonnie shared, "I see you having a Spiritual energetic expansion. The Spiritual energy around you is huge and sending out beautiful waves."

Dee chimed in next, "Keep writing. A book will emerge."

When I heard my information, I was excited, because all the information was accurate. Laurie touched on my writing. I had been journaling for twenty years or more. Bonnie tapped into all that had been happening with my emerging mediumship and my claiming my abilities to read the Divine Spiritual Energies. What also caught my attention were Dee's words, "*A book will emerge.*"

I had been given my first Divine Prediction about writing a book over fifteen years before this (the first story I shared with you in this book). This second book writing prediction reminded me that I had been excited about the possibilities of writing a book but hadn't come to any conclusions of what it would be about. I knew that if I wrote a book, I would include all the experiences around my mom's illness, death, and my healing afterwards. I just wasn't sure if that's what it would end up being about, and I knew I wasn't ready to write about it yet. So I tucked this information away like I had before and prayed that I would someday know more about what this book would be about.

The Divine messages I received that day helped me feel that I was on the right track on my Spiritual Journey. God had put me together with others who had similar gifts and desires to help people on their Spiritual paths and with their Spiritual evolvement. I felt I was exactly where I needed to be, and I was learning and feeling more confident with my path and my newly claimed gifts.

Also, in the summer of 2015, I found myself waking up with bits of wisdom for myself each morning. I placed a small notebook by my bed so that I could quickly write them down.

I grew to look forward to waking up and getting the daily wisdom. Most of the Divine messages were general in the beginning and were well-being and uplifting messages for the day, such as, "*All is Well*," and "*Follow Your Heart.*" I started calling them my Self Soul Readings and was fascinated with this new reoccurring experience.

At times, they were more personal and direct. "*Learn how to receive love.*" "*Love others. No need to solve their problems.*" "*Create your happy world.*" "*Rest in My love.*"

I sometimes asked direct questions about my life, wanting direction. One morning I shared, "My shoulders hurt." The answer I was given was, "*I am healing them and taking away your burdens.*"

Another day I asked, "My back pain, is it from my past?" The Divine answer was, "*Maybe it's wanting to stretch and grow pains.*"

Around this time, I had considered a joint venture with someone. I would get excited and then feel resistance about it. I wasn't sure why. So I asked, "Why am I feeling this way about this new opportunity?" My answer was, "*This is not your Soul's Purpose.*"

That personal reading really impacted me. I made a promise to myself to always check in with my intuition on anything that I thought about committing to, no matter how wonderful it sounded. That message compelled me to consider everything that I am asked to do. I decided if it doesn't align with my Divine missions, I must say no.

Give yourself time to sit quietly, journal, and answer important questions that you have such as:

- Am I fulfilling my soul's purpose?
- What is the purpose of a particular life event?
- What other questions seem important for you to ask right now?

What answers have you written down?

How do you feel about your answers?

Is there any area of your life that you want to change right now? Choose one area, jot down a few small action steps, and commit to taking action this week.

CHAPTER 20

My Mediumship Starts

A lot was happening the summer of 2015. I wanted to do more soul readings for people. I wondered how I would do it. I asked God for help and waited for answers to unfold.

Near the end of the summer, my friend and reflexologist, Sandy Praska, had an open house at her home and invited me to come. There were many wonderful women there, and I enjoyed meeting and visiting with them all.

Joan Johnston, a woman from Cresco, was sitting next to me, and we started talking. She shared with me that she was planning another holistic health fair in September of that year. Each year she had twenty-five vendor openings and breakout sessions throughout the day. Practitioners from Iowa, Minnesota, Wisconsin, and Illinois would be there. She'd been doing this for several years and had quite a good attendance.

Joan was interested in what I did, and I shared about doing Soul Readings. She thought that would be a great addition to her health fair. The idea of doing Soul Readings in such a large room, as it was being held in a former school gymnasium, didn't appeal to me at first. I needed time to consider it. She asked me if I wanted to be in her fair, and I said I just wasn't sure and wasn't able to commit at that time.

I was at home a few days later, and I had a big swirl of energy around me (I thought about Bonnie Winninger's reading from several weeks before), and I thought about doing the Soul Readings at Joan's holistic health fair. This surprised me, yet it filled me with such excitement and anticipation that I couldn't get it out of my head. I soon realized this was exactly what I had asked God for.

I called Joan right away, because I knew she had said she was almost full. She was excited that I had changed my mind and decided to do it. I also agreed to do one of the 30-minute breakout sessions, as someone had cancelled.

As soon as we hung up, I felt fear enter my being. I had so many questions about how this was going to go, what I needed to do, and I began to get overwhelmed. I had about two weeks to prepare, and I knew I needed to trust myself. For what I couldn't figure out on my own, I could call on Joan and, of course, ask God for help.

I am amazed how, when opportunity knocks, ingenuity and creation come together in magical ways. I believe we all come here to create—to co-create with God. And I've noticed that when I create, there's nothing like it. I feel focused, and I love brainstorming, with all its options. I love the feeling of intense focus and wonderment as decisions are made, played out, and results are realized.

I focused on my vendor table first. I knew that I wanted it to be inviting, yet simple, and convey that Soul Readings would be taking place at my table. I found a gold tablecloth that I used on my dining room table that would fit the dimensions on my vendor table perfectly. With a soft paisley background, it reminded me of energy moving in a swirl. I had a long, soft silk, magenta scarf with delicate fringe on the ends that I swirled around on the table. It signified beautiful Divine Energy to me, and the lovely gold and pink color combination made me giddy.

I wanted to have a form for myself to take notes on, because when I do a Soul Reading, I get messages that I want to share with the client, and I don't want to forget to tell them, as they might be sharing something with me at the time. I used yellow gold paper for that.

I also wanted to have a form for each client to take notes on and take home with them. I drew a flower with the petals listing all the areas of a person's life, such as their career, health and well-being, relationships, etc., and used pink paper for that.

Things were coming together, and it made me more excited. The health fair was on September 12, 2015, and my dahlias were in full bloom. On the day of the holistic health fair, I cut a beautiful magenta pink dahlia for the table. Perfection.

With the table design ready, I needed to decide what topic I was going to share with the fair attendees at my breakout session. I wanted to help the attendees understand how I was able to do the Soul Readings and what the benefits were. I left time for questions from the audience, as I believe people learn more quickly when they get their questions answered.

I wanted to remind people their soul is Divine vibrational energy that is connected to our Source, so everyone has access to Source/God. I wanted to inform them they all were resonating through Spiritual Communication, even though they might not be aware they were doing it. Spiritual Communication is something we all do each day when we make our choices by paying attention to what we resonate with vibrationally. Whether it's choosing our food, friends, books, TV shows, spouses, or careers, we make our choices by what we resonate with energetically and our unique preferences. We, as souls, have this ability to have Divine Spiritual Communication with God, our Source, and it is our first and natural form of language.

I also wanted to address the question, "Why communicate with your Soul?" I came up with answers that would assist listeners on their spiritual journeys. Some of the reasons I came up with were: responses from your Soul are for the highest benefit of all; your Soul can answer your most pressing personal life and business issues and concerns; you can receive confirmation on an inkling or hunch; your Soul can help you get unstuck; and listening to your Soul can save your time, money, and resources in solving problems. The most important reason for connecting spiritually is to provide us with a closer relationship with our Creator so we understand we are not alone and feel all the love, protection, and guidance we are being given.

I gave thirteen mini-soul readings that day, and the time flew by. I was filled with awe, and I couldn't wait to do more of them. I had asked God for the opportunity, been given the chance to help and teach others, and I also learned more about my Divine gifts in the process. I felt the expansion of my Divine gifts that Bonnie Winninger had told me was coming. I loved doing the readings and where my life was going. I felt relaxed, confident, and joyful with the readings I was giving. I marveled at everything that was unfolding.

In the late fall of 2015, I had a chance to practice my mediumship. Our son and daughter-in-law, Nathan and Candace Fober, had a neighbor and friend who had suddenly died. They were devastated. When I talked to Candace, their neighbor who had passed came through and wanted to share a message with her that he was fine and no longer suffering. As we were talking, her deceased grandmother came forward, as well, with a personal message of love and comfort for her.

It felt like a gift for me, too, as it had been about two months since I had told God that I would serve as a medium for people if He so chose. The entirety of 2015 was a time when I was adding building blocks, one by one, piece by piece, towards the culmination of my mediumship ability being realized. I was inspired, grateful, and humbled by all that had transpired.

What questions do you have for your Soul to answer?

What areas of your own life are you either stuck in or frustrated about?

Begin to ask these questions and notice what thoughts and answers come forth. While you don't need a medium to find your own answers, treat yourself to a session if you resonate with this form of Divine Guidance or if you are stuck or want to learn more.

In what ways are you using Spiritual Communication that you haven't fully acknowledged?

CHAPTER 21

Highly Sensitive

One day in January of 2016, I was awakened at 4 a.m. and could sense that I was being given a Divine message. I grabbed my notebook and pen and heard the Holy Spirit say, "*Call us Divine Guidance.*"

I was thrilled to get this message, as I had been wondering what to call this entity that was giving me these Divine messages. I was doing more Soul Readings and sometimes felt awkward about how to refer to the source of the messages. With this message came the awareness that Divine Guidance was referring to God, Jesus, the Holy Spirit, my spirit guides, my guardian Angel, and our loved ones' spirits—all in the Spiritual Realm. I now fully realized the spiritual team that was available to me. I am still in awe at the multitude of help that is available for us all.

The Holy Spirit continued, "*Live in the higher frequencies. We are trying to show you that your fear leads you into lower frequency living. Fear is just you not accepting who you really are—a Divine being. Judging yourself and others is a vicious cycle. Whatever you accept yourself to be, so it is. If you accept yourself as graceful and healthy, that is what you will get. If you accept yourself as clumsy and not healthy, that is what you will be. It's a choice of lower versus higher frequency living."*

I was excited, because this is what I had been sharing with my clients over the years. It always sounds so simple but isn't always easy. Yet when we practice staying positive, we create new habits, and those new habits create better results in our lives.

The Holy Spirit continued, *"Teach others what we are teaching you. Teach others to heal. Teach others to meditate. Teach others their soul answers are God's messages, Divine Guidance, being given to them."*

Wow, I was overcome with excitement and had a hard time getting back to sleep. I felt God knew exactly what I was doing. This message was a confirmation of that. I also felt it was encouragement to continue with what I felt was now my soul's mission in life.

It was also around the beginning of 2016 when I discovered Elaine N. Aron, PhD, and her book, *The Highly Sensitive Person: How to Thrive When the World Overwhelms You* (1996). I was 58 years old, and I began noticing how sensitive I was to light, sound, and other people's energy.

If my environment was too hot, too cold, too noisy, or too crowded, I could get overwhelmed and feel quite uncomfortable. I became unable to watch movies or TV shows that had a lot of violence in them. I had always been a very emotional person. Other people's moods affect me, and I am very sensitive to pain. Caffeine overstimulates me, so I stopped drinking caffeinated beverages.

If I didn't plan my day accordingly, I could easily end up overstimulated, have a headache, or feel drained. If I didn't eat often enough, I would feel stressed and overstimulated. I now carry nuts and dried or fresh fruit with me, because if an event or errand takes more time than I plan for, I can feel my energy draining, and know I need to eat something, or I will not feel well.

I always keep water with me. I need to stay hydrated, because if I don't, my energy drains. It's sometimes rather comical to others, but when I leave the house, I have an entire care package with me, including food, water, extra sweaters, hats, lotions, bug spray, etc. My husband has learned to help me plan and make sure I am ready with everything I need before he starts the car. My grandchildren love to be around me at soccer games or other events because they know I will probably have whatever they are looking for in my bag. I have learned to be prepared.

I noticed that others around me weren't carrying water with them, or noticing their hunger, or worrying about being too cold or too hot. When I would comment on such things, others would respond as though they weren't feeling what I was feeling.

When I read Dr. Aron's book about being highly sensitive, it was as if I had finally been seen and understood. I learned that approximately fifteen to twenty percent of the world's population is highly sensitive. Which means that the other eighty to eighty-five percent of the population is not as highly sensitive. Well, that explained so much to me about why I seemed to be the odd person out. I now understood why I was always trying to cope with what seemed to be perfectly normal circumstances for other people.

I am also highly attuned to weather. When the barometric pressure goes up or down, my sinuses can start draining. If it's a large jump either way, I can have quite the headache. I learned that many highly sensitive people get even more sensitive as they grow older, which has been my experience.

While this all sounds rather negative, and I do require extra planning for my well-being, there is an upside. Because highly sensitive people are equipped to take in more stimuli, we are the ones that can edit a document quicker and more accurately than most. We notice details, many times life-saving details, that might be missed by someone who is not as highly sensitive.

Dr. Aron's book was a game changer for me. I'd always tried to fit in, cope as best as I could, and tried to make excuses for my energy being drained. I often became overstimulated and didn't feel very well at gatherings. Many times, I would wear myself out by the end of the day but be so overstimulated that it would be difficult to wind down and go to sleep at a decent time.

After reading the book and learning about what I was dealing with as a highly sensitive person, I found the confidence to not apologize for taking care of my needs and was able to be a lot more compassionate with myself and others who were also highly sensitive. I also find myself doing the best I can to educate others to the reality of being highly sensitive.

I no longer consider it a burden, but a privilege, to be born with all that comes with being highly sensitive. When I try to do too much in a day, I pay the price of feeling drained and overstimulated, and I am reminded of the extra caretaking that I require. But when I understand what I need to do to have an optimal day and fully take care of my needs, it's gratifying and exciting to be so highly sensitive.

The advantages are many and amazing. If something is off, new, or different, I will pick up on it. Those who are highly sensitive make excellent detectives, event planners, chefs, leaders, writers, musicians, attorneys, doctors, scientists, inventors, and innovators. Those who are highly sensitive naturally become masters in their fields because of their ability to take in many times more details than non-highly sensitives. They synthesize and process these details into nuanced information that non-highly sensitive persons simply miss.

All my sensory abilities are acute, including my memory. While I have journaled through the years, and my notes have assisted me in writing this book, I can remember word for word most of the conversations and events that have taken place in my life, like they happened yesterday. Everything sensory that I do is an elevated experience. When I eat, it's tastes so good to me, and I am mesmerized by how amazing each meal is. Art, beautiful nature scenes, and flowers take my breath away. How things look, feel, and sound in my environment is highly important to me.

I also learned that those who are highly sensitive have been found to be highly intuitive, and many are blessed with elevated abilities in Spiritual Communication. Reading Aron's book helped me understand and accept myself in a way I had never done before. Everything made so much more sense.

Are there situations in your own life where you are particularly sensitive?

Take note of them and write them down. I encourage you to discover and embrace your unique sensitivities. See and claim them as strengths for your life.

CHAPTER 22

Florida Readings

Iled a coaching group down in Florida in 2016. Each participant chose their goals, and I coached them each week to support their progress. One of the ladies in the group, Sue B., age 81 and still a tennis dynamo, had lost her beloved husband, John, a year or so before. Her goal was to start dating again and find a wonderful man for a companion. She jumped in and scheduled three dates online in 10 days! I was so proud of her for her courage and willingness to act.

After several weeks went by, Sue shared in our group that she was not connecting with anyone and that she was frustrated. I picked up that she had an energetic block and asked her after the class if she wanted to have an energetic reading to help her take care of this, and she agreed.

The reading was at her home, and I immediately felt the energy of her late husband, John, once I arrived. It was a very loving and protective energy. It was obvious to me that she wanted her late husband's permission and blessing to enter a new relationship for love and companionship. Without it, the block would have continued to be in her way.

John came through for her, and shared that he wanted her to move forward, and that he approved of her decision to start dating again. Sue was so happy and relieved.

Loving someone new after a loved one has died will never take away from the love you created with your deceased loved one. Sue had tears of joy and comfort knowing that he would always be present in her life and there for her, no matter what, and would support her for the rest of her life.

This message allowed her to continue with a free and open heart, and within several months, she had found a new and wonderful love, and was thriving with this new man, while still enjoying the love that will never end from her deceased husband.

The highest form of energy is love. It is so comforting to know and experience that when a bond of love is created, it will never go away.

Also in 2016, I was invited to a neighbor's party, and I started talking with one of the women there, Pat. She asked what I did for a living, and I shared with her about my intuitive coaching and soul readings. She had never had a reading but knew of someone who had. Pat wasn't sure she wanted information because she was scared it would be bad. I shared with her that before I started doing this, I had similar concerns, but assured her that the information that I received was from God and Heaven, was always helpful, and that I didn't want to know any negative information unless it would be helpful to someone. She was relieved.

We started talking about something else, when suddenly I could energetically see a woman in the background, and she was looking through a magnifying glass at an older woman's chin, looking for chin hairs. I thought to myself, well this is crazy information, and I'm not sharing this. This is too wacky. I really couldn't understand why I was being shown this.

Suddenly, Pat said, "My mother was so funny in her later years before she died. She would always make me look for hairs on her chin, want me to get the tweezers, and pull them out!"

My mouth dropped open, and I shared with her what I had been experiencing. I was as surprised as she was. We both laughed so hard. This may go down as the craziest reading that I've ever had, and I learned my lesson. Never question Divine messages from the Holy Spirit. No matter how crazy they seem.

Also, that winter in Florida, I decided to do a small group reading in my condo, and six women had signed up to attend. I was excited, yet felt stressed out, because this would be my first group reading. I really didn't know if I would be able to pick up on everyone's energy accurately, with others so close by.

I decided to put an extra chair next to me, and when I was doing each individual mini-reading, I would have them sit next to me. That made me feel a little more comfortable.

I asked each of them to bring along specific questions that they would like to ask me. I find in a mini-reading, I like it when they have questions, because there's only so much time, and I want to make sure they get their most pressing questions answered.

The last reading I did was very interesting. Billie's questions were about a family member in another state. I began to sense that this family member was connecting to us energetically at the same time we were doing the reading and that this person was taking in the information at the same time as I was delivering it. I shared with her that this family member was also very intuitive and tried to explain a little bit more about what I was sensing. It was like this person was in the room with us. Then I shared with Billie that if she talked with this family member about the question she had asked me, they would understand everything that Billie told her, which she confirmed with me two weeks later, when I saw Billie again.

I was surprised at my confidence when I delivered this rather unique message, but as I continued to do readings, I knew I was learning to trust and not question the messages I received, whether they made sense to me or not. I trusted God with this gift that He had given me. I began to relax, deliver the messages in the best way I could, and trust they would be given for the highest benefit of all.

Gary and I had joined a ballroom dance group in Florida, and I went to buy some shoes for dancing. I found a pair, was getting ready to purchase them and check out, when it started raining. And this was no regular rain. If you've ever been in Florida, you know that they can have torrential rains, and it was coming down in sheets.

There was no way I was going to try getting into my car as I couldn't see anything but water outside. I didn't have anywhere else I needed to be, so I just laughed and thought, well, I will just relax and enjoy myself in this store.

I sat down, and the woman who had helped me came over and started talking to me. I got the sense that I was supposed to give her a reading. There was a male spirit present who I sensed was her dad. I told her I was a medium and that I felt her dad was with us. I asked her if her dad had passed and if she would like a reading.

She told me yes to both questions. She sat down with me, and her dad began apologizing to her for leaving her when she was a child. She was stunned and began crying.

Then I was told the pain that she was feeling because of her family was affecting her health and that it was time for her to heal. She began to share some of the major hurtful events that she had been through because of her family. I listened carefully and attentively. My heart went out to her for the pain that she had lived with for so many years. Her dad's spirit also listened and continued to apologize throughout her sharing. As she talked, the tears continued, and I thought to myself, well it's raining inside and outside today. Very fitting.

When our loved ones' spirits come through, many times there are apologies that never came during their lifetimes. Divine Guidance has shared with me that souls, when they are in Heaven, do their spiritual work, and they begin to grow and understand things they couldn't in their lifetime on earth.

While it is certainly heartbreaking, it is also an honor to witness how people can heal and find comfort after being given evolved and important messages from their loved ones.

I'm not sure how long I was in the store that day, but I was able to deliver and witness a transformation of healing, forgiveness, and love.

After a while, the woman I read was able to gather herself, blow her nose, and breathe easily again. I asked if she was ready to accept his apology and take better care of herself. She said she was. I could see how much this had changed her. She looked different. Her face was softer, and I felt like her breathing was more relaxed.

I shared with her that it takes time to heal, and she deserved to let herself feel however she wanted and needed to feel. I also told her that her dad would be listening to her, and she could talk to him anytime she wanted, and he would hear her.

Then it happened. The rain slowed to a sprinkle, and we both laughed a little. My work complete, I gathered my bag with my dancing shoes and waltzed out the door.

Do you relate to this story? Is there anyone in your life that you would like to have an apology from or have resolution with? While you may want to hire a professional medium, you can also know that your deceased loved ones are listening to you. You can talk with them whenever you want. Or try journaling in your notebook about how you feel about the situation. What responses do you sense? Write them down. Trust yourself with this process and notice how you feel. The more you connect with yourself and how you feel, the more you will strengthen your ability to notice when these deceased loved ones are connecting with you.

Part IV

Intuitive Readings
Transform Lives

CHAPTER 23

A Premonition for Gary

In mid-September 2016, I woke up with a premonition. This wasn't a premonition about something good.

There'd been a lot of rain in the area. The Cedar River had flooded. Gary had planned to go to Cedar Rapids that day. I had the premonition that something bad was going to happen to Gary, but I didn't know what it was.

There had been flooding in Cedar Rapids, with reports of electrical lines down, as well. I asked him not to go to Cedar Rapids, and he promised me he wouldn't.

I should've told him not to leave the house. Because while I was getting a reading from Laurie Hazel (see the next story), he decided to take a walk outside. When he was in the cul-de-sac, he tripped.

He fell on his left hip, which he had already had three surgeries on. NOT GOOD!

He was able to get up and didn't feel too bad, so he finished his walk. He came inside, looked at his hip, and saw he had a bad contusion.

He decided to take a shower and then drove himself to the ER at Sartori hospital.

I got his text message that he was in the ER as I was finishing up my reading with Laurie. His contusion was huge, about the size of a small football, the ones our grandkids played with when they were younger.

Thank goodness the x-ray showed that it had not bothered his hip replacement parts; that was a huge relief. He needed to stay off his leg for a while, so we had to cancel plans to take the grandkids out of town, but it was a minor miracle that the hip was still intact.

This is one time when I really wished I had been able to get more information about what might happen from my premonition. But that was all I had gotten. If there is a next time, I will probably have to put him under house arrest.

I learned to take premonitions very seriously that day. I've never really had one that was so negative that didn't include more information. It was hard to know what to do about it. As the years have passed and my intuition has proved accurate, Gary, and others who know me well, take heed when a Divine message comes through.

I was so excited to have my reading with Laurie, and I arrived with high expectations. What was interesting to me was that when I arrived, I energetically saw a very good-looking man with curly dark brown hair sitting down near us. He was in spirit form, and I could tell that she did not know he was there. This spirit seemed as though he was not deceased. I thought he might be her future boyfriend coming to give her a message.

I wasn't exactly sure what to do, so I just sat down and waited for Laurie to sit down with me. As soon as Laurie came into the living room and sat down with me, the male spirit moved to the back of the room, by the window. He was obviously very polite and was not going to interrupt what we were planning, and he was willing to wait, so I was fine with that, and my reading got underway.

Laurie started out by telling me that everything that had happened in my life had been important to my spiritual growth and evolution and that I had learned many lessons. She said that I was nearing the end of needing to heal anything else in myself, which I was very happy to hear.

She said that I was a very strong spirit and that everyone I interact with feels my spirit. She said people feel me, and it feels good to them. With that, she cautioned me a bit. She reminded me to ask for protection when I am with other people so that my energy does not get drained.

She talked about my health and said that I can just be my happy and healthy self every day. She shared that my mom and dad are at peace, their deaths were painless, and I can give all my worries to Heaven.

She also said that she knew I would be writing a book. This was now the third medium who had told me that. After my mom died, I felt like I would possibly be writing about her death and all the amazing things that happened during her illness and after her death, along with my own healing journey.

She then asked me, "What do you want to write about?"

At that point, it was the question I had been asking myself for over sixteen years. I still wasn't sure then, yet I had started thinking that I would be writing about all the Divine Intervention that had been happening to me, about all the Divine experiences I'd been having because of the supernatural gifts I'd been given by God. I wanted to write these stories down but didn't know if this was the book I'd been told I would write.

I told her, "I'm not sure yet."

Mom came through. Laurie said I was like my mom, always thinking of others. I had given Mom my pink raincoat several years before she died, and Laurie told me Mom had loved it. Mom wanted me to read to her what I was going to write for my book.

Dad came through. He said, "*Yeah, a whole house full of girls!*" I laughed because he said that with a bunch of girls and one bathroom, it was tough to get in there because someone was always washing their hair. He said that each of us girls was different, and it was never boring.

Then Mom came through again. She talked about loving to watch the grandchildren. Mom also said that she was proud that her kids all went to college. She sees us playing board games with the grandchildren, too.

The Angels said that my soft-spoken voice is a true gift to people and that I'm a good listener. The Angels thanked me for listening to people. They see me teaching others what I am learning. I am to keep doing what I am doing. I'm also good at questioning people.

She said Jesus wants me to write a book, and Jesus is going to inspire my writing.

The Angels also added that as I have helped myself to heal, I have helped others to heal, as well. I've gone through incredible growth, and they want me to know that they know it wasn't easy. But I chose to be a positive role model. Mom really helped me with that. I have healed trauma from several past lifetimes. I am to teach others to heal as well.

My two huge lessons to learn in this lifetime are patience and peace. The reason I had to go through so many lessons was so that I would be able to relate to people and understand their troubles.

The Angels said, "*We are proud of you. We acknowledge all the work you have accomplished and the growth steps you've taken. Thank you, too, for acknowledging yourself. You are daily divinely inspiring. We give messages to you freely and often. You feel and see us as well. Feelings are what Angels use to communicate with you most often.*

"*Know you truly deserve this time of peace and rest, that you will continue to serve and do good works, and it will be blessed. Call on us to help you with that, so our words come through you. We bless, thank you, and honor you. Amen.*"

After we finished my reading, the dark curly haired man who was present when we started, who had been sitting in the back of the room, had now moved so he was parallel with me.

I asked Laurie if it was okay to share with her what was happening. I told her it felt like I was supposed to give her a reading about this man who I was seeing.

She emphatically said, "Yes!"

I asked her if she was interested in dating and eventually getting married. She said, "Yes."

The man was sharing with me that there was a growth issue on her part that was energetically blocking this desire. I asked her about this, and she admitted she had a fear about being in a romantic relationship. It was then that I knew exactly what her fear was.

I said, "He is telling me that you are afraid to let down your walls and allow love into your life. You are afraid that something will happen to him, and because you will have lost such a great love, you fear living through that pain."

She said, "Yes, that's it exactly! How do you know that?"

We both laughed, as we are both mediums. Even as mediums, we are amazed at our ability to do these readings and sometimes wonder how it all happens. I just raised my head, turned my eyes towards Heaven, and said, "You know it's all Divinely given."

She said, with a gleam in her eyes, "Yes, I do know that!"

As a medium and intuitive, I am continually amazed and learn something new with every reading that I give and receive. That day, I learned someone who is currently living can also appear with an important message, and I am able to see them. So, it is possible for those who are alive to transport themselves energetically, for the highest benefit of all.

Also, three amazing and important experiences happened to me all in this one day. The premonition of protection for Gary, Laurie's reading for me, that included the third time I was told I would write a book, and the reading I gave for Laurie. It gives me pause and makes me realize how active and extremely loving and helpful our Divine Guides are.

CHAPTER 24

Manifesting Evelyne

In the fall of 2016, I was sitting in my office one day. Out of nowhere, I started thinking that I was going to meet a new friend with a lot of qualities and interests similar to mine. I couldn't see her in my mind's eye, but I could sense her.

By this time in my life, I had had lots of experiences with manifesting, so it was fun to imagine all the fun we would have. I could see us talking about our grandkids, enjoying each other's flowers, and running around together, having lunch and going shopping.

And then I forgot about it, as life got busy and moved me on to new projects and adventures. With manifesting, once you know what you want, are clear about it, and confident that it's on its way, you can relax and know it will show up in the perfect time. Manifesting is about asking for what you want and knowing that God and the Divine Energy System that He created are your partners.

A local hospital in town sponsors the Festival of Trees every year around mid-November. It's a wonderful five-day series of events for our community and a major fundraiser for the hospital. Individuals and businesses decorate trees for Christmas and sell them in a silent bid auction, and there are other holiday-related activities too. It's my favorite pre-Christmas event of the year, as the trees are so beautifully decorated. It always begins the Christmas season for me in the most beautiful and fun way.

So Gary and I arrived on Saturday to take it all in. It was like being in a stunning winter wonderland, and we wound our way around the trees. Saturday is also their big bake sale day, so I was looking at all the yummy, decorated treats, too.

I was standing near some trees, talking with some women close to the bake sale tables, when I saw this other woman walk up near me. We were both in awe of this one tree.

I looked at her, and we started laughing and talking, and I said, "Where have you been all my life? I have been waiting for you!"

We both stopped, looked at each other again, and laughed. I shared with her that a month or so ago, I was sitting in my office and started imagining this new friend who was coming into my life, and I just had fun visioning all about it and following the manifesting rules. I knew that my new friend would show up at the right time. And that time was today!

It felt like she was a kindred spirit, and we were Divinely brought together at this moment in this perfect way. She thought this was the coolest thing she'd ever heard, and we both couldn't get over it. We stood there having so much fun, looking at each other, laughing, and talking about how much we loved the Festival of Trees event. We were having our own private party right there beside one of our favorite trees. I looked up and thanked God for her.

One day, about a year later, when my new friend, Evelyne Jennings, was visiting me at my house, she was telling me about her family and how her biological father and mother had not ended up together. She hadn't seen her biological father since she was two years old. She had a picture of her biological parents together, taken when she was around two, but she never saw him again and didn't remember him.

Her mom remarried someone else and chose to rarely mention or talk about her father, so she really didn't know that much about him. She'd wondered about him throughout her life.

Suddenly, I looked up and saw a man dressed in an army uniform sitting to my right. I asked Evelyne if she could see this man, and she said, "No, why?"

I shared with her that when I see a deceased spirit, I like to check in with the person I'm with in case they can see them too. I told her that I thought he was her biological father, and she said, "Why do you think he's my biological father?"

I said, "Because he looks exactly like you, except he's a man. I can't believe how much your faces look alike!"

She told me that she had been told that they looked alike. She was startled, yet waited for me to tell her more.

He was dressed in an army uniform and hat, and Evelyne confirmed that he had been in the Korean War and stationed in Germany. I saw a chain around his neck, and he picked up the pendant on the chain. He first looked at me, then Evelyne, and pointed the pendant towards her, as if he either had a photo of her on this chain that he kept around his neck all the time or his dog tags were meant for her.

He wanted her to know that he never forgot about her and always loved her. I wasn't sure, but he also might have wanted her to ask family members about either the dog tags or a pendant with a picture of my friend, his daughter. He later married someone else and had more children, but he was making clear that day, when he appeared in my living room spiritually, that he wanted Evelyne to know that he always kept her in his memory and close to his heart.

It was a very emotional reading. I felt a big, intense love for his daughter from him; it was almost overwhelming. I still get emotional every time I think of that reading. The presence of forever unbroken bonds of love is always the reason that deceased loved ones come through with their important messages.

People often ask me what it's like for me to give a reading where a loved one comes through. It absolutely feels like the privilege of my life, especially if there were difficulties in the relationship. Many times, the person coming through wants to say they are sorry and make amends. Or they want to bring comfort where there is a very strong love bond between the two and the client has been suffering. I get to feel the love that the deceased loved one is communicating to me to deliver to my client. As overwhelming as it can be emotionally, I always feel honored and grateful that I was chosen to deliver the message.

I have read that it is very difficult for the spirit to appear visually to the medium. And they only do it when being seen is extremely important for the message being given to their loved one. In Evelyne's case, it was extremely important. Being able to see him clearly helped me identify who it was so I could deliver a complete message to his daughter.

CHAPTER 25

The Dragonfly Princess and the Manager

I heard my husband, Gary, say, "Did you get my text?"
I said, "What text?" Turns out, for some odd reason, Gary's phone wasn't working.

It was sometime in January of 2017, and we'd planned to have a fun day in Florida, stopping at one of the farmer's markets, finding a yummy outdoor place for lunch, then ending up at our favorite candy store as our finale. Pretty much a perfect day.

While it was a perfect day, in between the market and lunch, Gary continued to struggle with his phone. Knowing that I couldn't really help him, and as he continued talking with his cell phone company throughout the day, I was free to focus on what I had been struggling with: claiming my supernatural gifts—*all* of them.

I had been having conversations with myself about this issue over and over for months. I was frustrated and getting nowhere. I felt desperate and needed guidance, Divine guidance. I decided to take it upstairs.

My conversation with God that day went like this, "I'm so happy to be serving You in this wonderful way, and I love helping people with their life struggles and through their times of loss. But I'm scared. What will people think of me? Will they take all this the wrong way? I'm afraid my relationships would change with some friends and family members if they knew. You know how some people don't believe there are those that are gifted with Your supernatural gifts. And so many ignore and disregard their own intuitive abilities. Some people act like I'm a bit too much anyway, with my heightened intuitive abilities and sensitivity. You know what happens. They get quiet, their eyes start rolling, everyone feels uncomfortable, we move on to something else, and I end up feeling defeated. You know how much I hate to be rejected. All I want to do is help people and serve You."

There. I poured it all out: the good, the bad, the ugly scary, and the stuff I didn't want to admit. That's the thing about God. He lets you do that. He lets you be weak before he reminds you of your strength and His faith in you to do what's right to serve Him for the highest benefit of all, letting Him handle the naysayers.

I took a breath and waited.

The answer was clear, as His answers always were. "*It's time,*" I heard. Then, "*How are people going to know you can help them and others if you don't claim this additional gift I have given you and tell people you are a medium?*"

When God speaks to me through the Holy Spirit, I am always humbled.

I gave myself a silent pep talk to stop worrying about what others think. Besides, He was always right. I needed to keep my focus on helping people. God would take care of me and the non-believers.

"Ok, God. You are right, and I promise I will start telling people."

We had just arrived at the candy store, and I went to the counter eagerly. After my Divine Intervention sidebar, I was feeling like these calories from my treat were going to evaporate as I enjoyed every bite. Yep, I was feeling invincible.

I was their only customer. I noticed a beautiful, multi-colored dragonfly tattoo on the neck of the young woman waiting for my order.

"What a beautiful tattoo!" I exclaimed.

"Thank you. My mom and I got the same one together."

"That's so neat! I think some tattoos are so beautiful, but I would never do it because of the pain." I shook my head and shuddered.

She said both she and her mother never experienced any pain while they were getting their tattoos.

"That is quite a phenomenon! While I have never experienced that, I do experience other phenomena."

"Oh, what kind of phenomenon have you experienced?" she asked.

There it was—my open door. Would I go through it or hold back in fear again? I took a breath and said rather quietly, but clearly, "Well, I am a medium."

Her eyes opened wide, and her eyebrows shot up to her hairline. She covered her mouth as if she were going to scream. She twirled around and started looking in the back area of the shop. Suddenly, the front door swung open, and four customers walked in.

I thought, "Okay, I've scared her, and she's looking for the manager to throw me out."

I called out that I didn't want to bother her and went outside where my husband was waiting. He was still trying to get his phone to send out texts, so I sat there melting in the heat of the Florida afternoon, wondering what to do. When I saw the four people walk out of the store, I decided to go back into the air conditioning, and I promised myself I wouldn't bother the young woman. I would simply get my chocolate treats, sit down, and cool off. That's it.

I walked back into the store. Now there were two women standing behind the counter. The one with the dragonfly tattoo was pointing at me and jumping up and down. I asked God to please help me, as I didn't want to be in trouble.

As calmly as I could, I started reading the menu, trying to focus on the chocolate. The new gal said, "Are you a medium?"

I felt myself beginning to choke, but fought it, and said, "Yes."

With a big smile, the new gal explained she was the manager. I relaxed. I could tell they were simply hoping for a nugget of wisdom for their lives. I willingly obliged.

The dragonfly princess went first. I shared that I was being told she was a healer and that she should start the instruction she desired. She responded that she was hoping to become a nurse but had been hesitant about applying for school. She expressed relief and gratitude for the Divine confirmation she'd just received.

Then her friend, the manager, started talking. I interrupted her, "Oh, you have *two* questions for me."

She said, "How do you know that? Because I do have two!"

I smiled, pointed, and looked up. "I just know!"

I then said, "Okay, we'll start with the most important question in case twenty people walk in, and we have to stop the reading."

She said, "Should I get a divorce?"

I frowned. "That doesn't sound good or right."

Suddenly, to my right, a huge, beautiful female energy appeared.

I said, "Wow! Whoever she is, she has tremendous power and strength."

I felt my right-hand rise and point to the manager's husband as if he were standing there next to her. The female spirit was wagging my index finger at the invisible husband like he was in real trouble with her.

It was an accident. Not her fault. I shared what I heard the female spirit proclaiming.

The manager exclaimed, "Yes!" She started trembling and held her face in her hands. (Many times, a reading will feel like a rollercoaster ride, both for the medium and the person getting the reading as the pieces of the puzzle come together.)

I then kept hearing the name, *Bobby,* again and again, so I said, "I'm not sure what this means, but I keep hearing the name Bobby over and over—Bobby, Bobby, Bobby."

The manager paled, as if she had seen a ghost. "How do you know my son's name?"

I said, "I don't, but this female spirit does. She wants her son to start thinking of her grandchild and to stop blaming you—because you are innocent."

I pieced together that the manager had been in a car accident seven years ago that was clearly not her fault. She was driving with her baby son and mother-in-law in the car. The mother-in-law protected the baby in the car and died doing so. The husband blamed the manager for his mother's death. Bobby was now seven years old, and the manager had suffered under the relentless and misguided blame from her husband for seven long years. The best solution she could think of was to divorce him, break up her family, and try to stop the despair that was slowly strangling her.

I don't remember buying or eating the treats I took home that afternoon. And my husband did get his phone to start working again. But I'll never forget the dragonfly princess and the candy store manager. As the tears streamed down the manager's face, I remember wondering what would have happened if I hadn't shared my gifts that day.

I received my own gift that day. I believe God made sure that I would never consider hiding or denying my God-given abilities again.

I asked the manager what her second question for me was. She was still crying. She shook her head back and forth and said, "No, there is nothing else I need. You saved my marriage and my family. You saved my life."

As we hugged good-bye, I whispered in her ear, "God saves all of our lives."

I feel that entire day was Divinely orchestrated. God and the Angels were working their intricate timing and synchronicities, including my husband having trouble with his phone, which I felt was a key piece to the day's events. If Gary hadn't needed to spend time trying to get his phone to work, I probably wouldn't have felt as free to take the time to engage with the women in the store.

Even though I am given messages to relay to people that need Divine Intervention, I don't usually know the entire Divine production that is going on, swirling the miracles around us at every turn. But I have learned to trust God, Jesus, the Holy Spirit, and the Spiritual Realm. I continue to be filled with awe from all that continues to unfold.

I am an ordinary person who gets to be involved in the extraordinary workings of Divine Intervention because I want to help people and serve God in this way. By His design and creation, the continuous miracles provide healing, love, and resolution for people who are suffering and need them. When I wake up in the morning each day, I pray, "Put me in front of those You would have me help today, and I will do my best for them and You."

People ask me how I can live my life this way, but it is a way of life that fills me with joy and gratitude that overrides the fleeting times of fear or apprehension I sometimes feel initially when I'm giving a reading to someone. Also, I accepted my abilities to read Divine Energy from an early age. While I was quiet about it and had no vocabulary for it until I was in my 30s, when I started calling it all Divine Intervention, I was still aware and communicating with God and his Spiritual Realm daily.

Even though I might call myself a late bloomer to mediumship, I always felt the presence of my deceased loved ones since my late teens. I wouldn't outwardly claim all of this until 2015, but I, like you, have been Spiritually connected since birth. And I didn't let go of it. Through time, experience, and practicing getting clear on how to do this type of work, I have developed an ease and confidence that serves me, clients, and this Divine process well.

While we can never really know the difference our gifts will make in other people's lives or how they will be received, I was grateful I had decided to not hold back that day.

Are you holding back your Divine gifts? We all do at one time or another. But there comes a time when we must face our fears. I was afraid of what others would think. Some of us are afraid our gifts aren't good enough. We compare them to others and discount their value. We may think our gifts need to be practiced and aren't quite ready, or we are afraid of making a mistake.

But, when we focus on our fear, we're focusing on the wrong thing. Remember there are people who need your help and guidance right *now,* and they don't need you to be perfect. If you have been holding back, decide now to claim your gifts and take steps toward helping the people you were born to help.

CHAPTER 26

Clairalient and More

It was about 5 a.m. one morning in January 2017. We were in Florida, and I hadn't slept very well, so I didn't feel rested. It was too early to get up, and I was hoping that I could fall asleep again while I meditated.

Suddenly, I smelled the scent of lavender. It smelled so good and pure. I tried to take huge breaths of air, just because it smelled so good, and I could tell it was relaxing me. I looked around and wondered, where is this coming from? I use lavender oil and had it in my bedside table drawer, but it wasn't out, so there was no way the strong whiffs of pure lavender were coming from there.

So where was this smell coming from, I wondered? I began to sense my mom. Oh, it was such a wonderful feeling to know that she was offering this scent to me. I was amazed. I had read about people being able to smell scents when the real scent couldn't have been present. They call this psychic ability clear smelling, or clairalience. I have experienced four other clair senses: clairvoyance means clear seeing, clairaudience means clear hearing, claircognizance means clear knowing, and clairsentience, clear feeling. But this was the first time I'd ever noticed this spiritual ability, so I was very excited. There is also clairgustance, which means clear tasting. I have not experienced this yet, but because I am so sensitive to taste, I don't really care to have this one unless it would be the only way for me to receive a particular message to help someone.

Each person who communicates spiritually is unique and may use one or two of the clair senses more than others. Some will be able to actually see your deceased loved ones, and some will receive messages through knowing, hearing, or feeling. I utilize all the different ways, except for the clear tasting. That could change, depending on the spiritual energy that is being sent. With each reading, it's up to the deceased loved one who's bringing the message and the medium to connect so the medium can decipher the messages that are being given. My readings are unique and varied, and I never know which form of the senses I will be utilizing.

I was trying on dresses in a department store one afternoon while we were in Florida in 2017. I was standing in front of the mirror, looking at a dress I had just tried on, and I saw a woman walk into another dressing room. I picked up on some energy, but I wasn't sure where it was coming from, so I went back into my dressing room and tried on another dress.

When I came out to look at this dress in the mirror, the woman was now standing in front of the mirror, looking at the shorts she had just tried on. We started chatting about our shopping.

I was turning to go back into my dressing room when I began to sense a male spirit coming forward, and it felt urgent. Normally, I probably wouldn't say anything, but it just felt so important.

So I said, "I really hate to bother you, but I keep getting the sense that there is a young male spirit who wants to get a message to you."

She covered her mouth with her hand and looked at me in amazement. She said, "It's my son. He died last year. I had set up an appointment with a medium before we left to come to Florida, and she had to cancel it, as she was moving and ran out of time. I have been hoping, desperately, that I could find a medium, to help me get a message from him."

I gave her my card, wrote my cell phone number on it, and she said she would call me that weekend. Because I was meeting Gary soon, I said good-bye and drove home.

A couple days later, on Saturday, when I was getting ready to get up, her son's energy was present again, and he encouraged me to call his mom. Dana had given me her phone number, as well, so I had it, but thought, "No, she said she would call this weekend, and that will be fine. I will wait for her call."

When I got up Sunday morning, her son's energy was present again, this time urgently encouraging me to call her. I talked about this to my husband, and we agreed that if she wanted to call me, she would. She didn't call me Sunday.

Monday morning, once again, her son's energy was coming through, this time emphatically, trying to get me to call his mom. I debated back and forth. Finally, I gave in. I have this rule. If I get the same message three times, then I usually act.

I called her mid-morning on Monday, hoping I wasn't disturbing her. I shared with her what had been happening with her son's energy, and I said, "I'm getting the feeling that I might have given you the wrong phone number. Do you still have my card?" She said she did and went to get it.

When she came back to the phone, she explained to me that she had thought about calling me Sunday, but thought she'd wait until Monday. I asked her what number I had written on the card. After she told me, I said, "No wonder your son was trying to get me to call you, because I wrote my Iowa landline phone number down instead of my cell phone number. And your son knew you didn't have the correct phone number."

We both marveled at how he knew this. And then we scheduled her for her reading, so her son wouldn't have to try and connect us again.

Our loved one's spirits know the details of what's going on in the physical world. They try diligently to come through to ease their loved ones' suffering.

In February 2017, there were windy and dry weather conditions down in the Naples, Florida, area. My friend, Theresa, and I had decided to visit the Naples Botanical Center one day. In the early afternoon, I noticed bits of soot and small pieces of wood flying all over. There was a distinct smell of burning, and I could see black smoke in the air. I realized there were devastating fires just south of us, and I told Theresa we needed to get on the highway and drive home, *NOW!*

When we got on the interstate, heading north, the traffic was terrible, and we saw firetrucks, police cars, and other emergency vehicles driving towards Naples.

After we got home, I turned on the news, and found out that with the dry spell and high winds, fires were erupting and spreading. I immediately asked for help from God, Jesus, all the Angels, and every spiritual entity that could help. I asked for help in accordance with the highest benefit of all for the people, the animals, and property, and shared it with my friends on Facebook. I asked them all to join me in asking for a miracle to stop this fast-moving and devastating event. I went to bed that night hoping and praying for the best possible outcome, as thousands of acres of land, property, and animal and human lives were at stake.

In the middle of the night, the miracle happened. The wind died down and changed directions. Dramatically fewer acres were burned that night, and countless homes, humans, and wildlife were undoubtedly spared.

I was so thankful when I got up in the morning and learned what had happened. I continued to ask for prayers and miracles for this situation.

I sometimes feel helpless in these kinds of natural disasters. But then I remember the power of prayer, which falls into the third step of the Five-Step ACUTE System (the system introduced in Chapter 6 and summarized in Appendix 2 which helps us expand our abilities to communicate spiritually) for using Spiritual Communication. U stands for *Utilizing* our tools, such as prayer, to communicate our needs and desires to God and the Spiritual Realm. I remember the power that God has and His ability to create miracles. We have full access to our Creator, and Spiritual Communication is our lifeline to God. I am comforted to know that we can always ask for help by praying—our most foundational form of connecting with God.

Throughout *Opening to Divine Intervention,* you have read how I pray in almost every experience I've written about. Now you know why. I use the ACUTE System every day. This direct communication with God and your Divine Partnership is the best action you can take and has the capacity to create great miracles.

One of my clients thought she was asking God for too much and over praying. I shook my head and vehemently said, "No! Divine Guidance has shared with me that if anything, we are under-praying. Never discount the powerful frequencies of your spiritual energy and ask for help whenever you need it."

Albert Einstein said, "Matter is energy, energy is light; we are all light beings." This "light being" energy travels at the speed of light, which is 186,282 miles per second. Physicists agree on this fact. Spiritual messages are made up of electromagnetic vibrational energy and travel at the speed of light. That is why, when I'm doing a reading or talking to someone, I start getting messages within seconds. It is so fast, it feels instantaneous.

God has truly blessed us with a Divine Spiritual lifeline that is available for us in every moment, but it's up to us to *Accept* that Spiritual Communication exists, *Claim* it for ourselves and use it, *Utilize* the tools like praying and meditation to activate and strengthen our abilities to perceive and realize when we are getting Divine messages, *Trust* our feelings and the signs we are being given so we can interpret the messages, and *Enjoy* the process of Divine Spiritual Communication and the many benefits of love, protection, and guidance.

In May of 2017, I was talking with my client, Tina, and she was telling me that she wasn't sure she should go on vacation the first week of June. She'd had a job interview, and she was worried that if she got the new job, she'd have to start right away and have to cancel her vacation.

Without thinking, I told her she should go. I told her the job she'd interviewed for would not be filled until the middle of June, so she could go and enjoy her vacation. Which is exactly what happened. She came back from her vacation and found out she got the job in the middle of June.

When I find myself saying things like this, having complete confidence in a future event, sometimes I'm completely shocked. This is the kind of ability that I have had since I was a kid, and yet every time it happens, I am completely perplexed. I never know when it's going to happen; it just happens.

And when it does happen, I really don't even realize it. I'm just talking, and it comes out. After I say things like this, I always wonder, why did I just say that? How do I even know that? So, rest assured, I, too, wonder what just happened.

I'm at the point in my life now, though, where I simply accept it. I stopped worrying about whether it's accurate or not, because I don't know the last time when it was wrong. Besides, I can tell when advice is coming from me, when I'm figuring something out and sharing a helpful idea or tip. When it's Divine Intervention, I don't even know I'm saying it until I've said it.

I give all the credit to God and believe that everything I can do comes from gifts given by Him and His Divine Energy System. I'm simply utilizing the gifts.

I admire those who can learn foreign languages quickly and easily. Sometimes I wish I could sing better. I have no idea how my car works or how to fix it if it breaks down. I'm not built to do physical work in the building trades or withstand weather to work outside in all the elements.

I've come to understand and appreciate that we are each given our unique strengths, our bodies, and our minds. I seem to be equipped to read the energy frequencies of Divine Guidance and our loved one's spirits.

In I Corinthians 12, Paul, in his letter to the people of Corinth, talks about the Spiritual gifts given to people by God's Holy Spirit. We are all in this together, we all need each other, and we all need each other's unique and Divinely-given gifts.

I was doing a reading for a woman named Linda down in Florida, and she seemed frustrated. She couldn't figure out why she couldn't do energy readings and why she didn't have the abilities that I did.

I thought it was an excellent question, and I might have felt the same way she felt if our roles were reversed.

While I believe we all have been gifted with these natural abilities to communicate spiritually with God and His Spiritual Realm, we all don't always pay attention or have the same desires to use this form of communication. I have spent hours learning, meditating, practicing, and focusing on what I needed to do to be able to help people through Divine Energy Readings.

And I stayed open as a kid. I didn't discount what I was experiencing. I have been using the language of Spiritual Communication that we were given at birth for as long as I've been alive. I didn't always understand it or have words for it, but I was paying attention to it and allowing it in my life because it was always helpful and made me feel better. I was taught by my mother to pray daily, and I have continued praying every day of my life since I was two years old. So spiritually communicating with God and the Spiritual Realm is a way of life for me.

That's why I developed the Five-Step ACUTE System. I wanted to assist those who would like to strengthen their relationship with God and benefit from using their Spiritual Communication System that He designed for us.

I think most people disregard their intuition and Divine Intervention when it happens. I'm still trying to answer why I decided to accept and use the gifts that I have been given. But I think the better question is, "Why wouldn't I?" Because Divine Intervention and communicating spiritually have been some of the most extraordinary moments of my life. And when I experience how much they help me and others, it feels unbelievably good. And I always felt it all came from God. Always.

I believe everyone is born with the Divine gift of Intuition. Intuition has always seemed natural to me, like the ability to sing. I didn't learn to sing when I was a very young child, I just opened my mouth and started matching the sounds that my mother made when she was singing, then I sang all the time when I wanted to, by myself. Later, I did take singing lessons and learned more about music in chorus, but I did that because I wanted to learn more and improve my natural ability to sing.

I think people are Divinely gifted at birth with these abilities and their own interests. What makes someone want to become a doctor, a singer, a tailor, or a race car driver? I think it's a combination of the Divine gifts they were born with, plus the experiences they have along the way that they resonate energetically with. People have their abilities, and then they must add their desires, drive, experiences, preferences, and give it their best shot, hopefully along with a huge dose of Divine Intervention along the way.

I shared with Linda that I was sure she'd experienced Divine Intervention, but she probably wasn't aware of it or didn't remember it. She kept saying she hadn't. Finally, I asked her incredulously, "Do you mean to tell me that you have never experienced something you couldn't explain, ever, in your life? That Divine Intervention has never touched and helped you—in—your—whole—life?"

It got quiet. I waited.

Those words, asked in that way, must have unlocked something in her memory bank, because she finally spoke these words, "Well, there was that one time, when I was eight or nine."

I said, "What happened?"

She went on to tell me that she was mailing a letter one day, and a man in a white van got out of his vehicle and told her he had something he wanted to show her inside the van. Then she heard these words, out of the blue, "*You are in danger! Run!*"

And she did run, all the way to her house. I'm happy to say she made it home, safe and sound. This example of Divine Intervention, and the fact that she listened to it, might have saved her life.

I thought it was an incredible story of love, protection, and guidance, and an incredible example of Divine Intervention, but she had put it out of her mind and almost forgotten about it. Until I questioned her, she had no current awareness of or gratitude for what happened that day. That made me sad. If we can't feel gratitude for all the times we've been Divinely helped, protected, loved, and guided, I believe we've lost our way. But in that moment of remembering and recognition, Linda discovered a new perspective about her life and found something to feel grateful for.

Sometimes, we need a Divine reading. And, sometimes, we all need our memories jogged to help remind us that we are being Divinely cared for and watched over.

Do you have any memories of Divine Intervention that you haven't thought about in a long time? I invite you to write them down in your notebook and add the approximate date or time period when they happened. You might even consider creating a complete chronological timeline to give you clarity and that you can refer back to. You can add to it whenever you want, as your memories are revealed—or new Divine Interventions occur.

CHAPTER 27

My Face in the Sky

January 1, 2018, was a very special day. When I think about it, I can hardly believe what happened. I was awakened at 6:00 a.m. and thought I'd lay in bed and meditate, like I do almost every morning. Somewhere around 6:45 a.m., I felt a strong urge to get up and went out to the lanai. Around 7:00 a.m., I realized that I would be able to see the sunrise. I got excited and thought, what a great start to the new year!

Still in my pajamas, I put on my light pink hoodie sweatshirt with *Sanibel* across the front, grabbed my cell phone, and went out the front door of our Florida condo. The sunrise was spectacular, so I started taking photos. I had a dozen photos of the sunrise. I could see the shapes of Angels with giant wings in the clouds, too.

After the sun rose, I felt a strong urge to stay outside and watch the sky. I saw cloud shapes of hearts, more Angels, and a very large Jesus begin to descend and touch the earth's surface out on the horizon.

I was amazed and couldn't believe what was happening! I even saw the shape of a butterfly in the clouds. It was as if the Angels and Jesus were providing me with an incredible show—for my eyes only. I loved just watching the clouds move. I felt hypnotized by all the beauty and changing forms shown to me that morning.

After a while I didn't see any more distinct shapes, so I stopped taking photos and put my cellphone down on the concrete balcony. But I was still enjoying the sky, being outside, and the beautiful start to 2018.

Then I heard the Voice say, "*Start taking pictures!*" By this time in my life, I had no intention of not following through with this directive. So I picked up my phone and started snapping away. It was so strange, because I really didn't see anything of interest while I was doing this. Not in the sky or through the camera lens. So I stopped for a while.

But I heard the Voice again, and it said to keep taking the photos, so I did. All in all, I was outside over an hour, and I took forty-two photos.

After I came inside, Gary was up, so I showed him my photos while I went to get something to drink. I started looking over his shoulder as he went through the photos.

Suddenly, I said, "Gary, give me the phone!"

I took the phone and began to see something in some of the photos that I couldn't believe.

I saw my own face—in the clouds—in about four photos! I looked them over again and again and then asked Gary to look at them to see if he saw anything.

He exclaimed, "I see your face—in the clouds!"

I was rather beside myself and didn't know what to think. But every time I looked at those four photos, I saw my face, wearing my glasses, in the sky.

I started going through the other photos, and in certain ones, I could see letters—capital letters. It was a message in the clouds—a Divine message.

Gary and I spent the next hour, over breakfast, looking at these photos. We both saw capital letters that spelled out three different words in several of the photos. One was *FOBER*. Yes, those letters spelled our last name.

We also saw *STORY* and *SHORT*. I believe that I was being given a message from Jesus to help me get going on my book—the one that I'd been told I would write by *three* different mediums. I still felt confused and overwhelmed about the whole idea of writing the book, and this seemed like a message of support and help.

It felt like the messages in the clouds were telling me to write the book about my Divine Intervention experiences as if I were simply telling someone a *short story*. This beautiful Divine Intervention experience helped me relax and start seeing the writing of my book as simple and doable.

I have put this example of Divine Intervention into the Divine Natural Phenomena category. Have you seen clouds in the sky or messages in other natural environments that seemed to be a Divine message for you? What was your experience? How did it make you feel? How did it change your life?

CHAPTER 28

Full Circle

At the start of 2018, Gary decided he wanted to start reading the
Bible. I was excited for him and for the both of us. He liked sharing
the verses he had read with me each evening as we came together for
dinner and to talk about our days. It was always interesting to hear what
he had to say, what he related to, and what challenged him.

One day, he walked into my office and said, "I have something to
show you. You are going to want to read this."

I was deep in thought, and I didn't really want to be interrupted
right then.

He said to me, "Open up your Bible to 1 Corinthians, Chapters
12 and 13."

I gave in, reached for my Bible, opened it to 1 Corinthians 12 and
read the chapter. It begins with, "Now about the gifts of the Spirit…"

After I read the chapter, I was in shock. I looked at him and stared.
He stared back at me.

Finally, Gary said, "Do you know what this means?"

I said, "Yes. It means that what I and others have been doing, that so many are either frightened of or think is wrong, is written about in these very Bible passages."

He said, "Yes."

We sat there for several minutes, taking in the significance of what Gary had found.

I had just read about Paul telling the people of Corinth about all the spiritual gifts that are given to people. Whether it is the gift of spiritual wisdom, knowledge, faith, healing, the working of miracles, prophecy, discernment of spirits, or teaching. And that all the gifts are connected and important and needed for the whole. And that we should strive for these greater gifts if that is our desire.

I felt a veil of uncertainty lift from my body. Instead of hiding or worrying about what people thought, I now had a confirmation from a most powerful written source that my gifts were real and from God.

How could I be sixty years old and just finding this out? Was it still such a hush-hush issue that I'd never heard a minister, or even another medium, talk about it? Was it like a needle in a haystack that those in power didn't want anyone to find? It even says we should "desire" these gifts, which is even odder, as I don't remember anyone ever talking about this.

Reading this section of the Bible changed my illusion that our Spiritual gifts are something to hide or worry about others finding out about. I felt relieved. Now I felt I could fully claim the Divine gifts I had been given and feel wonderful and excited about them.

While I still have unanswered questions about why there isn't more mainstream knowledge about Spiritual gifts, I decided to not let it deter me from my work and missions. I decided to receive the words that I had just read with the gift of acknowledgment, accept it as the confirmation that it was, and use it as a powerful reference for those who needed it. Thank you, Paul, with your letter to the people of Corinth, for clarifying this.

And then 1 Corinthians 13 gives the highest impact, reminding us that without a sincere intention of love for our Creator and for people while we are using these spiritual gifts, then our gifts lose their significance and meaning.

I feel the timing of Gary discovering the confirmation of Divine Spiritual Gifts from the Holy Spirit in the Bible was significant for me. It gave me courage to keep going, with a Holy resource and reference to point to when I might be faced with rejection or naysayers about my expanding spiritual gifts.

It had only been about three months prior, at the end of 2017, when I truly felt that I needed to write down and make a list of all the Divine Intervention experiences that I was trying to keep straight in my memory. I still wasn't sure what the book was supposed to be about; I just knew I wanted and needed to get some of the wonderful miracles and Divine Intervention experiences down so I could see them in writing, understand them a little better, and put them in order.

So, when I got that sheet of paper and made my list, I couldn't believe I was coming up with so many. They flowed out of me onto the paper. I kept writing, just to see what I could come up with. When I listed out thirty entries with my first attempt, I was flabbergasted!

I had no idea I had that many stories to share. It was as if there were so many of them I couldn't hold the awareness of how many there were in my brain. They would pop out at various times, here and there, and I diligently added them to my list. I was thrilled as I headed to Florida with fifty of my Divine Intervention experiences on a sheet of paper. Then I had that amazing Divine moment (that I shared in the Introduction) when I was sitting at my desk and a powerful surge of Divine Energy pulsated and connected them all, and I finally realized that this was what the book was going to be about—all my Divine Intervention experiences.

As I was compiling my stories, I began to realize that there were times in my childhood and earlier life where there were significant moments that I believed were also examples of how Divine Intervention affected my life. So that's what's next. I wanted to take you with me on my journey. As I revisited my childhood and significant points from the earlier parts of my life, I had added insights from looking back at them as an adult. It felt right to include them here, and I hope you enjoy the full circle journey with me.

So, back to my childhood and the early years....

Part V

Child of God—My Early Years

CHAPTER 29

Meeting Jesus

There is a home movie that I'm in, when I was around two years old, and I have viewed it a couple of times. Nothing seemed significant about it until I decided to write this book on Divine Intervention. As I was creating my book outline and deciding what stories I would include in the book, this home movie kept popping into my mind.

At first it made no sense. Why was I continuously thinking about this movie? I really didn't know. So I decided just to play out in my mind what was on it and why it might be significant.

In the movie, I'm outside walking around on our front lawn. Suddenly I stand still, looking up and to the right, towards the sky. The movie isn't that long, but after I stop and look up, I don't move for the rest of the movie. I'm fully engaged and focused—looking up and to the right.

I kept going over and over in my mind why this was significant. What was I possibly seeing, and why was it important to the book?

And then it finally dawned on me. When I do soul and medium readings, I look up and to the right. That's how many of the Divine messages come to me. I look up and to the right. Hmm.

This felt significant because I have read that children arrive on earth highly intuitive and many times communicate with their deceased loved ones, Angels, God, and Jesus. You'll hear parents talking about their young children carrying on conversations with their special invisible friend or their deceased grandparents or siblings.

I have no way of knowing what I was doing in that movie when I was two. But because of all the Divine Intervention I've experienced throughout my life, I do strongly wonder if I was communicating with either a deceased loved one, Angels, or Jesus while the camera was rolling.

The fact that I was intuitively led to figure out the significance of this movie leads me to strongly believe that this was a very early Divine Intervention in my life.

As soon as I was old enough, probably around four or five years old, I attended Sunday school and church every Sunday, with a week of Bible School in the summers, all at our local Methodist Church.

This was a true highlight of my life. I'd gotten to know God and Jesus through the prayers my mom would say with me every night before we went to bed, but this time spent in church was my chance to really learn about Jesus and turn my relationship with Him and God into a true partnership and friendship.

I felt I certainly had already relied on this Divine partnership through my prayers and hearing my mother and grandmothers talk about God and Jesus, but this was like actually meeting Him through the songs, Bible verses, and stories. Hearing other teachers, leaders in our Church, and the minister added to my understanding through the years.

Singing was my favorite activity. Mom had us singing early, so early that I probably learned to hum tunes before I could talk!

My mom started working at the Cantril Bank when my twin sister, Kathleen, and I were two years old. When we were tall enough, we would stand in the back seat area of the car (no seat belt laws before 1960), with our little hands and arms hugging our mom as she drove us to the babysitter. We loved belting out songs like *Jesus Loves Me* and *I'll Be a Sunbeam for Jesus* the whole car ride. Other favorites were *This Little Light of Mine* and *Jesus Loves the Little Children*.

Then there were the Bible stories. I'm sure I wasn't listening all the time, but I was a kid who listened most of the time. After our Sunday school lesson, I remember thinking about what I had just heard and learned, and I tried to assimilate it into my six-year-old brain. I would even ask my mom questions when we got home about things I hadn't quite figured out.

These are my spiritual roots. I was a tender child of God. Tender in mind, body, heart, and soul. I was thirsty to experience the goodness/ Godness of this Divine relationship that just seemed, to me, to be the most wonderful thing that I'd ever been told about and given. When things didn't go my way at home, which, when you are the youngest, seems like always, or at school, I relied on God and Jesus to get me through. While I did feel alone and misunderstood sometimes, I could always rely on my spiritual relationship to give me some peace and help me feel better. When I reminded myself to talk and pray to God and Jesus, I always felt loved, heard, and not alone.

So, I didn't really mind being by myself because I knew I wasn't alone. And I could feel the Presence of God all around me. Growing up on a farm and being outside a lot of the time, there is so much beauty to see and take in. Grass, flowers, and crops grew miraculously. I had animals and pets to take care of and pet. I had a black horse named Beauty, a mixed border collie, Jack, and many barn cats that were my friends, too. Anytime I was down, I relied on them. I would bring Beauty an apple if we had an extra one. If we didn't have any apples, I'd go anyway just to visit her, pet her velvety nose, and look deep into the dark pools of her liquid eyes. With Jack by my side, a kitten or three in my arms, and God, Jesus, and all the Angels in Heaven up in the sky above me, I felt happy, content, and very blessed.

Do you have moments from early in your life where you remember having feelings of being totally loved and cared for by a Divine Presence? Describe your memories and write about them.

CHAPTER 30

Early Gifts

When I was around five years old, my paternal grandmother, Dora Bell Harryman, told me, "Oh, Karoleen has the secret!" I remember wondering what she meant. Being five years old, I took her literally. I shook my head no. I didn't have the secret. I remember her looking at me in a knowing way and staring at me like she knew something I didn't. I really didn't know what she was talking about. She didn't say anything more, so I just shrugged my shoulders and moved on.

But all these years later, I can look back and wonder. Was she also someone who had heightened intuitive abilities but chose not to share that with her family or maybe anyone? Those were times when most people didn't talk about things like that.

My Grandma Harryman took time daily to read the Bible and receive its guidance for her life. How blessed I feel to have had a woman like this as my grandmother, modeling reading the Bible and sharing it with others. She was someone who lived her close relationships with God and Jesus openly, for all to see. Her Bible was always close by, and the pages were worn from use. This focus of her life inspired me and influenced me greatly in my own life.

When I was five and in kindergarten, there was always some free time at the beginning of the school day before the bell rang.

I remember large, round tables that seated five or six kids each, and sometimes the kids would sit at the table and do puzzles or look at books as they waited for the bell to ring.

Sometimes, I found myself visiting each table during this time and talking with each of the kids. I asked them questions, listened to what they said, and responded to each one with lightness and fun. I was genuinely interested in each of them. It was like touching base with them to see how they were doing that day, and I remember encouraging them with whatever they weren't sure about.

This memory is the one that I shake my head about. It's like I was doing an energy reading or coaching session with my classmates as we started our day—when I was five!

One day when I was seven or eight, my twin sister, Kathleen, and I were at Grandma Morrow's house when Grandma said, "Girls, I want to talk to you."

Kathleen and I looked at each other, wondering what she wanted to talk to us about. So we went into the living room, and Grandma sat across from us and said, "You two are the smartest kids in your class."

At this statement, Kathleen and I looked at each other again, because we weren't sure that was a true statement.

I tried to correct her and said, "I don't think that's true...."

She was having none of my correction. In fact, she repeated what she had said previously, "Girls, you are the smartest kids in your class."

We just looked at her, not knowing what to do or say. So we did and said nothing.

Then she said, "And you two are the nicest kids in your class."

Well, with that, Kathleen and I looked at each other and nodded, and we both said, almost together, "Well, that might be true."

And then she said, "Don't forget what I just told you."

We said, together, "Okay, Grandma."

With that, she stood up, smoothed her apron over her dress, and went back into the kitchen.

Kathleen and I still talk about that incident to this day. Grandma never did anything like that ever again. In fact, Grandma Morrow was a woman of very few words and didn't really talk that much. So, when she did talk—we listened.

I really have no idea why she did that. It would've been around 1965 when this happened. Women had only been voting for 45 years. Maybe she just had a conviction about it and delivered it. We never talked about it again. She never even referenced it again.

There was a kind of a respect and reverence for grandparents in those days, and I didn't really ask them what they meant when they said something or talk to anyone else about the things they said. It was more like they talked, and I listened and accepted whatever they said, at least for that moment.

Her words may have been some of the most important words that anyone ever said to me. Throughout my life, when I have taken on new projects, new commitments, changed careers, moved, made decisions about relationships, and on and on, her words have drifted towards and around me, like a Divine message, reminding me of who I am, that I can accomplish anything, and I can do it by treating people well.

Maybe I will find out someday in Heaven what spurred her to make that momentous speech to us that day, but for now, I say, "Thank you for your words, Grandma. They have served me well."

Maybe the most important job I ever had was when I was around ten.

"Oh, no!" I shuddered. I looked at the clock. It was 10:30 a.m. I could feel myself go into my higher alert state. I tried not to panic, so I closed my eyes and repeated what I had to do: finish cleaning up the kitchen, set the table, peel the potatoes, all the while telling myself, today I will get it—the weather report. I will find the right radio channel, at the right time, and I will remember to write that weather report down.

It was the summer of 1967. Mom was at work at the bank. Dad was in the field baling hay with the hay hands (guys in high school who worked for my dad in the summer, baling hay for our livestock to eat). In the next hour, I would work on preparing lunch, try not to burn the boiling potatoes or frying hamburgers, and try not to get too distracted. I had to keep an eye on the clock.

To this day, I still can't remember exactly what time the weather report came on. I think it varied, which was why this task was nerve-racking. To the best of my recollection, the weather report was given somewhere between 10:50 and 11:00 a.m.

That darned radio scared me. It was always on a different station, and with juggling three or four other balls in the air, I was usually in a panicked state. It didn't help that Dad kept telling me how important this piece of information was to him. He made a lot of decisions concerning the farm based on what the weather was going to be. I always felt frightened that I would miss it.

And I had missed that stupid weather report plenty of times. Sometimes I burned the potatoes, or the potatoes would boil over, *and* I would miss the weather report. That was always a *really bad* day.

While I was slightly happy Dad trusted me to do this critical job, the fear of missing it, with so much on the line for him, was devastating to me when I didn't get it.

My reality was that I had to stop whatever I was doing, go to the dreaded radio, and hope I found the right channel when they were delivering the weather report. I was too afraid to tell Dad that I really didn't remember what channel he told me it was on. So for ten minutes, five days a week, for two summers, I turned the knob back and forth, listening hard for the right newscaster, hoping to hear weather words as I tried to turn that knob to the right station.

And when I say, "listening hard," I mean listening like my life depended on it, which it seemed like it did. Dad had a short temper, and when I missed it, he wasn't happy.

What's so significant about this bad-dream stage of my life? And why would I include it in my book on Divine Intervention?

Because the hard listening that I did for those two summers for ten minutes each day is how I feel when I start to receive a Divine message. Certain pieces of the message are delivered, and then I try to figure out what these pieces of information mean. I listen with great focus, the same way I listened for those weather reports. Only when I'm delivering Divine Guidance messages, the dread and angst don't happen. I'm still intensely listening, and it feels very similar, but without any of the fear and trepidation.

While I still refer to the radio weather report days as a relative nightmare, I feel grateful for those ten minutes that my ten-year-old self hunted for the weather channel, because, maybe, by doing it over and over again, it somehow helped my future mission in life—channeling Divine messages. I am learning that everything that happens in our lives is valuable, but it's up to us to figure out how.

Do you have Divine Pivotal Moments in your early life that seem significant and connected to your current life and mission today?

Did an experience that you considered negative in the beginning turn out to help you later in your life?

Did someone say something to you that helped direct your life?

Did you resonate with a particular situation or activity in your past that is directly connected to who you are today?

CHAPTER 31

Christ and *Kung Fu*

In 1969, when I was twelve years old, my parents were invited to a church service in another community that was giving a music concert as part of the service.

I remember the minister asking the congregation, "Who wants to come forward, up to the front of the church, and give their life to Christ?"

When I was a kid, I was shy and timid at times, especially about volunteering myself to be in front of a group of people. I was the kid in grade school who would volunteer to give my oral book reports first just to get them over with, so I could relax. If I didn't, I was so nervous, I couldn't focus on what was happening up front, and I missed everyone else's reports.

When I heard the minister ask that question, I rose instantly and started side-stepping out of the pew where I had been sitting. I couldn't wait to get up there.

I was in a connected-to-God zone. I wasn't thinking about anything that I feared. I was thinking, "Yes, I love Jesus so much that all I want to do is connect with Him." I wanted to give myself to the kind of love relationship with Him that I had experienced in every step of my youth. Jesus was my refuge. I prayed to Him every day, and I felt He heard and answered all my prayers. He was the best friend I'd ever have or hope to have. I felt I was loved by Him, understood by Him, and now I was being asked to give my life to Him. I wanted to do that. I didn't have to take time and consider it slowly or debate it, and I wasn't thinking about all the people I would be standing up in front of.

I was so happy that this was a possibility, that I could give my life to Him. I knew this was exactly what I wanted to do. There was no hesitation.

When I got to the front, I wasn't the only one. There were about twenty people who stepped forward that day and said, "Yes," too. I can't remember what the minister said to all of us. I just felt close to Jesus.

I went back to my seat in the same state I'd been in when I went to the front of the church. I was so focused on giving my life to Jesus that I don't remember seeing anyone's face or thinking about anything but how pleased I was with my decision. I felt it was the best decision I had ever made—and I still do.

During high school, one of my favorite TV shows was *Kung Fu*. I watched David Carradine as Kwai Chang Caine, a monk who travels through the American Old West, armed only with his spiritual training and his skill in martial arts, as he seeks Danny Caine, his half-brother.

In one episode, Caine was captured and put in an enclosure that was designed to torture him from the extreme temperatures of heat and cold (*Kung Fu* 1973).

Because Caine was a trained Energy Master, he was able to endure in the enclosure without suffering; he used his Divine Energetic abilities to overcome his reality. I thought about how God has given us the power to focus our energy on whatever we need and want to.

This Divine Energy training episode stayed with me. When I was in college at Iowa State University, laying out in the sun with my friends, it popped back into my brain.

"I should try my Kung Fu moves," I thought. Because there we all were, ten coeds, suffering outside on our blankets to get the proverbial suntan. Every five seconds, one of us moaned about how hot it was.

I closed my eyes, remembering the Kung Fu episode. I visualized myself not experiencing the heat and imagining feeling cool. I visualized myself in air conditioning, sipping a refreshing iced tea. It didn't take long. I was soon feeling cooler and more comfortable.

I started talking about what was happening, and I encouraged some of my friends to try it. They just rolled their eyes and yelled, "That's crazy, Karoleen. That won't work!"

I laughed and said, "Well, it won't if you don't try it!"

I let them razz me all they wanted. They just weren't taking me seriously. But I was out there getting a suntan and feeling like I was in an air-conditioned spa.

Our thoughts are powerful. Thoughts are made up of energy, and that energy has frequencies that, when directed, help us reach our desired intention.

In what ways—big and small—have you changed your circumstances because of how you focused your own Divine Energy? Have fun with this and list as many as you can think of. Don't be surprised if your list is longer than you thought it would be. Reconnect with the Divine Energy that you are made up of and use this to focus on what you want in your life now.

CHAPTER 32

Car Accident Miracle

On November 30, 1984, I had a car accident on my way to a meeting in Waterloo, Iowa. It had snowed, but the highways were well cleared. I was traveling about 50 mph in a 55 mph zone. I saw a car traveling on a side road up ahead on my right, but I knew he had to stop at the stop sign. There was a large building that obstructed my vision of him as he got closer to the stop sign.

Something told me that this guy wasn't going to be able to stop, but unfortunately, I ignored my Divine inkling and put it out of my mind.

I started thinking logically. I figured he couldn't be traveling that fast, and there would be no way that he would hit me. I thought I would be past the intersection before he got there, whether he stopped or not. I also worried that if I tried to slow down, I might hit some ice and lose control, or if I slowed down, then I would be at the intersection at the same time he was.

What I didn't know was how fast he was going or if it was slick where he was, because the building blocked the view.

Once my car was struck, I first had the sensation that my car was spinning, then everything went black. I had no memory of anything after that and still don't. All I know is that when I came to, I thought I was dead. Then I heard my radio, and I thought, "Great! There are radios in Heaven." When I came back to reality, I realized that my car was moving ever so slowly on the wrong side of the road going in the opposite direction from where I'd been heading, maybe a quarter of a mile from where I was hit.

I saw a man walking towards me. I finally realized I needed to stop my car, so I pushed on the brake and put the car into park. I tried getting out of the car, but I couldn't move. I finally realized my seatbelt was holding me in. I unfastened it.

The man was now up to my car, and I felt like he was the guy who had hit me. I asked him why he hadn't stopped at the stop sign. He just shook his head and walked away from me.

I tried getting out of my car but realized the door was locked. I unlocked my car and thought about getting out of the car, but I felt dazed. I felt almost paralyzed, so I just sat there watching him walk away from me.

After a while, a sheriff came and talked to me. He asked me if I was all right. I said I thought so. I told him I was late to a meeting in Waterloo, and he told me that I probably wasn't going to make it to that meeting. I knew I needed to make a phone call, and he said that I could call from a house nearby.

I got out of my car, and I could see the house the sheriff was talking about. Another woman who had stopped to see if she could help went with me to the person's house. They let me make a quick phone call to my manager, to let him know I'd been in an accident and was unable to make the meeting.

I came back out and was walking to my car when the sheriff came back to check on me.

He asked me where I lived, and I said, "West Union."

He said he would drive me home. I said I couldn't leave my car there, and I felt like it was drivable.

He said, "Are you sure?"

I said, "Yes."

He said I could follow him into West Union, and I agreed to do that. Little did I know what state my car was actually in. From the driver's side, you couldn't see much damage.

As I started driving, I couldn't figure out why it was so cold in my car. I wasn't driving very fast, so I started looking around my car. There was glass everywhere! It was then that I noticed that both the rear windshield and the right back door window were gone. I hadn't noticed it, nor had anyone bothered to tell me.

I was in shock, and freezing, but I did make it back to West Union. I decided to stop at the grocery store, as I was completely out of food, and I just remembered that my friend was coming to visit me that weekend. One of my friends, who worked at this grocery store, saw my car and wondered what happened to me.

I drove to my apartment, unloaded the groceries, and went inside. Two of my neighbors saw my car and thought I was dead! One of them knocked on my door to see if I was there and to find out what had happened.

Events happened so fast that day, and so much had gone on after the accident, that I wasn't able to think through what could've really happened. In fact, it was twenty-eight years later, and after my mother's death, when my intuition started talking to me and asking questions. What happened to my car after it was hit, while I was blacked out?

From how and where I was hit, my car should have been totally off the road, in a field somewhere, not on the highway slowly drifting in the opposite direction than I'd been going. Enough of the details weren't making sense to me that I felt like some form of Divine Intervention had helped me that day. I felt like my maternal grandfather, James Archibald Morrow, was involved in helping me somehow, so I asked Carol, my medium friend, about this.

She confirmed that it was a male descendant with Gaelic ancestry. My grandfather was born in Ireland and had died in 1970. She couldn't confirm which Irish descendant it was, but I felt an amazingly warm feeling of love float over me and through me when she confirmed that, in fact, I had received an amazing gift of Divine Intervention protection and love that day from my deceased loved one.

This Divine Intervention experience taught me an important lesson. I now do my best to listen to my Divine inklings. I'll never know if I could have prevented this accident, but I was given the information before it happened. I believe it was a miracle that I was not harmed in this accident.

Do you have a miracle story of your own? What happened?

Sometime in 1985, I was stressed out from work and had a severe neck ache. I drove myself home from work carefully, as my neck was so stiff, I could hardly move it. I got home and laid down.

My twin sister, Kathleen, called, and I told her what happened with my neck. She reminded me about the book she had gifted me several years earlier, called *You Can Heal Your Life*, by Louise Hay (1984, 1987, 1999). It was two feet away on my bookshelf, and I grabbed it and opened it to "Neck Problems." For each disease or body issue, the book gives you the probable thoughts that created the issue, then it gives you a new affirmation to repeat that replaces the negative thoughts. The negative thoughts that created the issue of neck problems were "Refusing to see other sides of a question. Stubbornness, inflexibility." I started laughing, even through my pain.

I really hate it when I get in my own way. I had to admit that there were some issues at work that I was being stubborn about. I was busted. I was being inflexible.

I thanked my sister for the great reminder and gift and told her I was going to say these new affirmations and rest, so we said good-bye.

I started repeating the new and better thoughts. "It is with flexibility and ease that I see all sides of an issue. There are endless ways of doing things and seeing things. I am safe." I said this over and over out loud and then in my mind over and over as I settled down to rest and fell asleep.

I woke up a couple hours later and had no pain! There was a little stiffness left, so I just kept saying the new mantra, and by the end of the evening, it was as if I had never had the neck pain.

That was my first real life example of healing myself, almost instantly, with what I learned and practiced from Louise Hay's book. It's become a staple in my life, and I have gifted this book to many others over the years. I have a copy of this book in my car, in several rooms of my home, and it is downloaded on my phone. I literally never go anywhere without it.

Our thoughts and feelings have their own energy frequencies. What are examples you have experienced where a refocusing of your energy has improved your life and well-being?

CHAPTER 33

Husband Prediction

In the spring of 1986, I was 29 years old. I went to a holistic spirituality fair. A woman was doing mini-readings where she had an outline of a body on a white piece of paper. She took crayons and began to color the different areas of my body represented on the sheet of paper.

She colored my hands green, my legs brown, my stomach red, and my head yellow. I had no idea what that all meant.

She said the colors were symbolic. Green hands meant that everything I would touch would be very abundant and successful, both in helping people and financially. My brown legs meant that I was a very strong person foundationally, and that no matter what happened to me in my life, I would be able to handle it and make it through.

The yellow colored on the top of my head meant that I was strongly connected with my spiritual relationship and that this would influence me greatly throughout my life, which has always been true.

She said that my red stomach meant that right then, I was very angry with a person and a situation. She was right, as I was having issues with someone at the time. This person was like a dictator and was always coming up with rules and ideas to try and control me and the others in the group I had joined.

I really valued my freedom, and I felt this person was overstepping her authority by telling me and the others in the group what we should be doing. I was angry, and I didn't know how to deal with it.

The woman who was doing my reading asked if I wanted some ideas to energetically handle it, and I said, "Yes!"

She said to go as close to this person as I could, or to an area where she normally would be, or even imagine her in my mind. She said to create a ritual where I would cleanse myself of her energy and control, throw it back on her, and declare to her and the universe that I was done being micromanaged by this person once and for all.

I was so excited to create this ritual that I went home that day and visualized the person. I went through the ritual and threw all that negative energy back at her in my mind and took back my own energy and power. I felt so good after I did that. While she tried to continue harassing me and others, after this exercise, I was never overly concerned about her again. I realized she had no power over me.

I asked the woman with the crayons about my love life. She said that I would marry a tall, dark, and handsome man with three children. When I asked her when this would happen, she said probably not for seven or eight years. I was not happy about that, as I was twenty-nine years old then and thought I was ready, and I didn't want to wait that long.

Oh well, I thought, even though I was actively dating people here and there, I hadn't really met anyone who I thought was that special, someone I could see myself growing old with.

I pretty much forgot about all of this until years later. I was cleaning out some files in my home office and came across the sheet of paper she had completed. I realized she had been totally correct. I started dating Gary seven years after her prediction, and I married him in 1994, eight years after this reading. He is 6'3" tall, had dark hair, a dark tan, because he is outside a lot playing golf, and he has three children. Oh, and about the handsome part? Yes, he is very handsome!

One year when I was a financial advisor, I hired a new assistant to help me with my workload. John was super nice, very conscientious, but there was one problem. He was making too many mistakes. I had been reading about manifesting and how to change your life energetically, so I thought this was a perfect situation to use what I was learning.

I sat down with him and asked him how he thought things were going. I could tell that he didn't have enough confidence, and he kept saying that he knew he was making a lot of mistakes. I interrupted him and shared with him that I thought he was, maybe, the best assistant that I'd ever had.

He looked at me like I was crazy. I went on and told him that I knew in the future, once he was a little more comfortable with everything, that the mistakes would stop, that he would be able to correct them easily and quickly, and that there was nothing to worry about. I again assured him that I had confidence in him, and I still felt strongly that he was probably the best assistant that I had ever had. And I added that if he had any questions about anything, to just ask, and I would help him.

I was amazed, because after about a week, he seemed like a new and much better assistant. He took his work seriously and seemed calmer and more confident. I'm sure he still made some mistakes, but everyone makes a few mistakes here and there, and he was able to get them corrected before he delivered the final product back to me. I was thrilled for both of us. Staying aligned with positive energy and teaching other people how to do it for themselves has always been remarkably easy for me and almost always successful.

I think back to my Grandma Morrow sitting me down when I was six years old and telling me I was the smartest and nicest kid in the class.

I give her so much credit for teaching me these skills early and expertly. That was my grandma practicing the best Divine Energy management and manifesting skills ever.

Think back to your own life when you changed an outcome because you realigned your energy to a positive frequency. Make a list of your experiences. What situations in your life now could use a shifting to a more positive outlook for a better result?

Part VI

Prioritizing My Spiritual Relationship and Mid-life Transformations

CHAPTER 34

Barbara and Namaste

Throughout the 1980s and 90s I started reading a lot of books on spirituality, and was attracted to authors like Louise Hay, Wayne Dyer, and Neale Donald Walsch. They wrote about their own spiritual journeys, their direct relationships with God, and our Divine Energy System.

You Can Heal Your Life (Hay 1984, 1987, 1999) is still my go to resource for metaphysical healing work.

I could probably write a whole chapter on how much Wayne Dyer influenced me with his tapes, books, and humor. Wayne was fun and zany. He made me laugh, whether I was listening to a tape or reading a story. And with so much fun going on throughout what he shared, I always came back for more and learned so much along the way. I felt so good when I spent time with Wayne Dyer's offerings and often shared with others how much his work meant to me.

Neale Donald Walsch captivated and inspired me with his story of his down-on-your-luck life circumstances in his *Conversations with God*,

Book 1 (1995, 1996). I related to him because I had been having my own ongoing conversations with God, as well. When you think you are the only one doing things like this, you can feel a bit alienated from others. When I find others who are doing things similar to what I'm doing, I feel I've found a kindred spirit and made a meaningful connection.

After I entered the world of life coaching, I did an exercise in one of my classes. I was given one hundred different words describing things that a person would value, such as health, money, art, creativity, music, humor, etc. The directions were to eliminate words until you were left with the top ten words that you valued most, and then to keep going until you landed with the one word most important for you. My top word was *connection*.

I loved these authors because I connected with them and what they were sharing. I found myself resonating with their experiences. Reading these books filled me with joy, excitement, and meaning that rang true for me and made me feel so good.

Somewhere around 1994, I became friends with Barbara Suzanne Morton (when I first met her, she was using her then husband's last name, Iversen) at my Methodist Church. She had been consciously walking her spiritual path while I had been on my own spiritual journey and yearning for a stronger and more direct connection with God.

I wanted to learn more about Barbara's journey and discovered that she was highly interested in the spirituality of indigenous people. She lived with various tribes in Africa in 1992, spent time with the Lakota of South Dakota, and did a ministry in Appalachia. She started seminary in 1993, where she completed her research on the common threads that ran between the Christian Holy Days and Celtic earth-based spirituality. She also focused her studies and research on the Christian Mystics, those who had experienced direct and Divine mystical experiences throughout history. She finished seminary in 1994 and began Namaste, a contemplative interfaith ministry that provided spiritual guidance and a holy space for individual and group experiences for those who desired a deep and intimate relationship with God.

I found Barbara accepting and welcoming to me and so many others, as we each discovered our Divine gifts and bloomed in this sacred time and space of acceptance and love. Through Barbara and Namaste events, I met multi-talented Light Workers who I continue to respect and lift up for their commitment to serving others and God, with the bonus of many becoming dear and trusted friends.

It was the perfect community for me to grow in, share and practice my gifts, and become more of who I was meant to be in my walk with God. I will always be grateful for Barbara's love, efforts, and the many gifts I received from her. So many of us grew and blossomed within her care.

I believe that we are Divinely offered people, places, and resources to help and support us on our spiritual journeys. What books, resources, people, and communities have provided you with support on your path?

CHAPTER 35

Spiritual Direction

I had been complaining to my husband for a couple of years about how bored I was in my business as a financial advisor. As a creative being, like we all are, I was ready to spread my wings, even though I wasn't quite sure what my next step would be. I would learn later, from the world of life coaching, that complaining about anything is a sign you need to change something.

And I was really torn. I had worked with some of my clients for fifteen years, and I adored them. Many of them had become my friends. It's easy to get close to clients, because they share everything in their lives with you. I knew about their health, their children, their grandchildren, their careers, their goals and dreams, and what made them laugh. I had no idea when I started my career in 1983 how much I would love it.

And over the years, I told my financial advising clients, with complete confidence, that I would be doing this my entire career.

And then one day, things changed. I remember walking one of my clients out to their car, and they said that they hoped I would never stop doing what I was doing. I assured the client that I would be there for as long as I was working.

And then it happened. I realized that what I had just said was no longer true. That as a creative being, I was ready to expand my abilities and find something that I resonated with in new and different ways. It was a feeling I had had for the last couple of years. And I was tired of ignoring it. If I was really going to be honest with myself and follow my soul's path, I knew I needed to start thinking about making a change.

Gary encouraged me to sell my practice to him and move on to something else that would address my longing for something new, something I could be more passionate about. He was tired of hearing me complain, too.

Gary and I had that conversation somewhere in the first part of November 1998. We figured out how to do it: I called all my clients, shared my decision with them, and thanked them for their business, confidence, and trust in me through the years. I explained that I was a little surprised with this decision myself, but I knew it was the right thing for me. I've discovered that using words like *never* and *always* isn't a good idea. You can't control how you will evolve from day to day and year to year.

And, as I have always been a bit protective of my clients, I couldn't have chosen a better advisor for them. I was excited for them to work with Gary and had such admiration for his education, experience, expertise, and who he was as a person. He truly was and is the best of the best, as a financial advisor and human being. Plus, I joked with them, as his wife, if he messed up, they could call me, and I would personally handle it!

Six weeks after we started our conversation, I sold my practice to Gary, and I was done. When all the paperwork was complete, and I had a chance to take a breath, I sat at my kitchen counter and cried. The career I had known and loved was over. I felt the bittersweetness of it all, the loss of the day-to-day contact with people I had grown to love and care about.

Because I now had more time on my hands and no clear next career move lined up, I decided to offer spiritual direction readings for people, and I also volunteered to lead some of Namaste's activities.

I thoroughly embraced my desire for continuing my own spiritual journey, and I was highly interested in supporting others to do the same. I also continued reading different books that interested me and that I resonated with. I love reading books, because it's such an intimate experience, and you can do it anywhere. It's a wonderful way to contemplate your own yearnings and experiences and process them through someone else's experiences, thoughts, and ideas.

I led several small study groups where we explored and shared our spiritual journeys.

I also found doing spiritual readings for people was a wonderful way to practice my knowings, my intuitive abilities, and have a direct and meaningful impact in people's lives. Little did I realize that this work would become part of everything I would do for the rest of my life. I learned that whatever you resonate with is what you should be exploring and spending time doing. Our inner beings are wise, and it's important to listen to ourselves and the Divine inklings and hunches that we have—and follow them.

All these experiences provided me with wonderful opportunities to jump in and explore my varied interests at the time, and I was most grateful. It also gave me a chance to meet many people who were on their own spiritual journeys with varied talents, skills, and modalities. I made many friends who are still friends today and learned a new respect for our unique abilities and interests. Meeting all those Light Workers created a new category of friends in my life, and they became my new tribe that I was thrilled to be a part of.

What times in your own life have you *known* you needed to make a change for yourself, even when you didn't have a clue how? Did you trust these Divine knowings and take small and large steps that led you to something better for you?

CHAPTER 36

Heal Michael!

I was exercising on my mini-trampoline one morning in 1999 when I suddenly heard the words, *"Heal Michael!"* I started crying, got off the trampoline, and sat down.

My friend Michael had recently been diagnosed with cancer, and I felt like I was being asked to heal him. I felt perplexed and overwhelmed.

How was I going to heal Michael? This question came into my mind over and over.

I told Gary about it right away. I needed somebody to talk to about this, because it felt too big, too impossible, and too crazy. Gary always listens to me, keeps me calm when I get wigged out, and then responds with simple and caring advice.

We'd been married five years at this time and shared everything in our lives. He knew about all the Divine Intervention experiences I had had through the years. He understood me being uncomfortable about all of this, even though I took it very seriously.

I told Gary that right now it was all very overwhelming to me, and because I didn't know what to do about it, for now, I would wait and see if I received any more messages.

I thought about this Divine message that I had been given every day. When you receive words like that, and truly would like to help but don't know how exactly, it nags at you. I started praying and asking God to help me with this request. I really didn't know what else to do.

Michael had shared with me a while back that his doctors had told him that he could possibly live a maximum of ten years.

I felt pressure to do something, but I told God I didn't know what to do. If I was supposed to help him heal, He was going to have to help me. I was exasperated and lost. All I could do at that point was trust that at some point I would hear more about what I needed to do.

A couple of years went by, and Michael wasn't getting any better, and I felt the pressure to do something. One morning, I woke up from a dream, and I was directed to call and talk with Michael. While I was frightened, I trusted my Divine dream, and I called him up and scheduled a meeting with him at his office. I didn't really know what I was supposed to say to him, but I tried quieting my nerves. In the dream, I had been Divinely told that I would know what to do once I talked with him. This made me nervous, but I trusted that God would not let me down.

I made some notes of some things I thought would help him visualize his health returning naturally. I used Louise Hay's book, *You Can Heal Your Life* (1984, 1987, 1999), as a reference for affirmations to heal cancer and had written down the affirmations and my own thoughts to share with him.

I was a wreck on the drive over to his office that day. I had left in plenty of time, but because I was so nervous, I drove past the driveway to his office.

I arrived a few minutes late and apologized as I sat down in a chair across from his desk. We chatted a little bit just to catch up. He was in good spirits, and even though I was scared, I tried to relax. I didn't share with him about the Divine directive to heal him or about any of the interactions or Divine Intervention experiences I had had. I didn't want to distract either one of us from just sitting together and allowing whatever was going to come.

I started by asking him how he had been doing with his health diagnosis.

When he started telling me about how his father had died from the same diagnosis and how he figured he would die from it too, my whole body felt like it lit up. This was the sign I had been anticipating; it's when I knew I was supposed to help him change his thinking. I told him that this belief was a problem. And that he needed to change his thinking.

In fact, I was being told Divinely that he needed to delete that thought immediately and never think it again. I shared this information with him by simply telling him that I was getting a Divine intuitive message about his situation. He seemed a little bit startled when I told him that, but he instantly composed himself and listened to me with a serious look on his face.

He told me he was absolutely resonating with what I was saying, and he promised me that he would never have that thought again. He also said he would visualize his body completely healing.

I was overjoyed and relieved and sensed that I had delivered the Divine message that I had been asked to deliver. I also sent him healing thoughts whenever I thought of him for the next year or so.

I am happy to report that the doctors told him a year later that he was completely cured. I'm also happy to write that he is still alive, an additional fourteen years after his maximum ten-year life expectancy prognosis.

Ideas and beliefs carry energy. Ideas and beliefs affect how we live our lives and the health of our bodies. When I am working with clients, I always look out for ideas and beliefs that are detrimental to people's lives.

What negative ideas and beliefs do you carry that aren't in your best interest?

Spring of 2000 found me taking a senior level art class at the University of Northern Iowa, and we had a spring break week coming up. Gary and I decided to take a road trip where we just followed our noses.

One night in a hotel, I had a vivid dream. I woke up in a sweat. In the dream Gary and I were in a place where there was broken glass everywhere. The dream jolted me awake and warned me to be careful while we were on our vacation.

I told Gary about the dream. We didn't know what to do about it, but I told him that I thought we should be careful when we entered any building on our trip, and he agreed. A couple days later, we were walking into a restaurant. I began to feel a little strange, so I started looking around and moving more slowly. I told Gary that I felt a little strange, but I couldn't see anything or sense what exactly might be wrong. He told me he didn't notice anything.

A server led us to a table. And that's when I saw it—all the broken glass! Broken glass was everywhere—on the floor and on the table. Who knows if we would've stepped on a large piece of glass or placed our hands or arms on a piece of glass if I hadn't been given this dream.

They immediately moved us to a different location, and we were fine. I told Gary that was what my dream from several days earlier had been about. This was the Divine Intervention warning that I had been given to keep us safe and unharmed from the broken glass. Gary just shook his head up and down, nodding yes.

Have you had Divine dreams that helped you or warned you of something to avoid? These are messages of Divine love, protection, and guidance, given to you for your benefit.

In September 2000, I was at home straightening up the house. It had been almost two years since I had sold my financial advising practice, and I still wasn't sure what direction I was going to go in.

I rarely turned on the TV during the day, but I was coming into our master bedroom, and for some reason I just sat down on the bed and turned the TV on. I flipped through the channels and saw that Oprah was on and stopped there.

Her guest that day was a woman named Cheryl Richardson, and she was talking with Oprah about something called life coaching.

I listened for a while and said to myself, well I have been doing this since I was five years old. And people get paid to do it! I was so excited; I started researching life coaching that day.

I had been searching for a new career, and here it was. I had been Divinely led to turn on the TV.

This is what I love about Divine Intervention. You never know what you're being led to, but it almost always turns out to be helpful or point you in the right direction. Why did I turn on the television? Because I got a Divine impulse to do it, even though that wasn't my usual behavior. And I've trained myself to recognize, accept, and follow these impulses. Sometimes Divine Intervention is so subtle, we don't even realize it when it's happening. We are led to reach for a certain book, turn the television on at a certain time, call someone, or sit next to someone at an event, and our lives change. Once you become more aware of what is *really* happening, you will be more open to paying attention to your Divine impulses and following them.

Do you notice your own Divine impulses? How? What do they feel like?

Jot down a quick list of those times when you felt you were being given ideas or being led to do something that seemed unusual or important to do, yet you weren't sure why. How did these Divine impulses impact your life?

Take a few moments to describe more about these experiences in your notebook. Consider connecting with these memories and allow yourself to focus on them. Then as you move back into the present, stay aware of these kinds of impulses, and try to notice them when they occur. Connect with them with appreciation and look forward to them. Open yourself to recognizing them as beautiful gifts as they are happening.

Part VII

Manifesting and Creative Endeavors

CHAPTER 37

A Kiss from Wayne Dyer

I checked out life coaching online and found out there were national conferences. That year's 2001 conference for the International Coach Federation (ICF) was in Chicago in the summer. I decided to attend this conference, and Gary came along with me. The speakers were fantastic, I met some new friends throughout the breakout sessions, and I could see and feel that these people, who had all come together to embrace life and business coaching, were my people.

I met several mentor coaches who I was drawn to; I got their contact information so I could talk with them further once I returned home and got organized. I was pumped!

We arrived at the airport early for our flight home. We were visiting with another couple, and I shared with them about attending the coaching conference. We were interrupted by an announcement on the loudspeaker that told us our flight was delayed, and possibly canceled, because of a plane repair that needed to be completed.

I heard the groans from weary people just wanting to get home, or to their next destination, and get back to their lives. People were complaining and trying to figure out what to do.

I wanted to get home, too, but I waited a few minutes. Then I had the best idea. Let's manifest the plane getting fixed perfectly and quickly and all of us getting to our destinations with only a minor delay.

I shared my idea with the couple we were sitting next to. I shared that I use manifesting in my life all the time. We could sit there and complain, think the worst, and be grumpy. Or we could follow the rules of manifesting and start visioning how our plane was being fixed, that they would fix it perfectly, and that we would all get home with only a minor delay.

The woman of the couple started laughing and said, "I love that idea!" She talked her husband into doing it, too. He mostly watched, but she and I took turns talking about how great the repair people were, that they were getting the parts they needed, and that the plane would be ready to go shortly. We really had fun, and we were giggling. Yes, right there in the airport, we were having a very important and happy manifesting party.

Okay, I admit that there were some other people wondering what the heck we were doing, but we didn't care. It was fun, and what else was there to do? Gary figured he had some time, so he went to get a snack. But this woman and I, we held the floor, and we held the Divine Energy in its most desired frequency. We kept talking about how happy we were that everything was getting fixed and how we'd be on the plane soon.

Twenty minutes passed. We were still nodding our heads yes, and we were winking at each other and smiling the whole time.

And then it happened. Twenty-five minutes from the time they announced the delay, the loudspeaker told us the good news, that we would all be boarding shortly.

The other woman and I jumped up and hugged each other. We knew we had rocked it, and I told her that I was going to remember how much fun we had together manifesting our plane getting repaired in record time.

On the morning of September 11th, 2001, where were you? I was upstairs at home, exercising. My husband yelled my name and told me to turn the TV on, which I did.

Nothing could have prepared me for what I saw as the Twin Towers tumbled down. I couldn't believe my eyes. I was so horrified that I turned the TV off after only a couple of minutes.

I dropped to my knees and immediately started praying. I asked God to help all the people who were in this horrific situation. I was breathing fast, and my mind was racing.

I intentionally slowed my breathing, closed my eyes, and found my center. I placed my thumbs and index fingers together on each hand. This yoga hand position allows you to breathe from your diaphragm, stops stressful chest breathing, and reduces further stress on your adrenal glands and immune system. It works if you are doing this with only one hand, too, if you need to drive, eat, or take notes when you are in a meeting.

I started praying again. It had been a couple of months since I'd returned from the ICF coaching conference. This was my wake-up call. I prayed and asked God to help me move forward with coaching, as I knew the world needed it from what I saw that morning. I was scared, but I was also ready and willing to serve.

This was a Divine Pivotal Moment that moved me into taking action. What Divine Pivotal Moments have you had, and how did you take action?

As I've mentioned, one of my favorite authors and spiritual leaders was Wayne Dyer. I have read many of his books and listened to his tape series over the years. I had always wanted to meet him.

In 2002, I was at the International Coach Federation annual conference in Atlanta, Georgia, and I shared with some other coaches how much I loved Wayne Dyer. I went on and on about him and half-kiddingly told them I was probably going to meet Mr. Dyer very soon. I shared with them that my husband and I were planning a trip to Florida in a few months. I knew he lived in Florida, so I was telling everybody that we would simply have to meet and go out for lunch.

My new coaching friends kidded me and laughed at me, and I told them, "No, seriously, I expect to meet him very soon." Sure, he didn't know me from Adam. Sure, I wasn't going to call and tell him I would be in Florida in a few months. Yet I had a strong sense that we would meet, and I felt confident when I shared this with people. Yes, I will tell you, a few of the coaches rolled their eyes as they listened to me. I didn't let that bother me, however.

The conference went well, and it came time to fly home. We landed in the St. Louis airport with a tight connecting flight home. I had slept on the plane from Atlanta and was groggy and tired from our early flight. As I got off the airplane, I was following my husband and not really looking at anyone. We were on one of those moving sidewalks that make you walk faster than you really do, when, over to my right and just ahead, I heard a voice that I recognized.

I shot to attention and turned my head to make sure I wasn't just hearing things. There, a mere ten feet away, walking in the opposite direction, was none other than Wayne Dyer! Mamma Mia—my dream was going to happen in the St. Louis airport. In fact, my dream came true two days after I said I would meet him.

I yelled to Gary that I had just heard and seen Wayne Dyer, and I was going to follow him and meet him. My husband just muttered and shook his head. I must tell you that my husband absolutely knows how much I love Wayne Dyer, and he knew there was no talking me out of it. Gary simply kept walking and told me he hoped I would make the connecting flight and that he would see me at home.

Once I got off that machine, I turned the corner and basically did the 60-yard dash to catch up with Wayne. Anyone who knows Wayne Dyer knows that he doesn't rush as he's walking if he doesn't have to. He strolls. So, I caught up with him very quickly. I was now practically walking beside him, and I said, "Excuse me, are you Wayne Dyer?"

He stopped, turned, smiled at me, and said, "Why, yes!"

We had the most wonderful conversation. I shared how much I had enjoyed listening to his tapes and reading his books through the years and how much they had helped me. I tried not to swoon, but that was impossible. Before we parted, he leaned down and kissed me on the right cheek, and we hugged as we said good-bye. Meeting Wayne Dyer was one of the most wonderful moments of my life and one of my best manifesting experiences of all time. And I made my connecting flight home, too.

Using your energy by speaking what you desire and sharing it with others is very powerful. In fact, I learned that *abracadabra* is the Greek word for "I create as I speak." And I learned that from none other than Wayne Dyer.

What are you creating with your words?

CHAPTER 38

Healing Touch

May 7th-9th of 1999, I took a 20-hour Healing Touch class. Penny Hanson, another woman I met through the Namaste community, provided our training, and she did an excellent job. She was patient, clear, and thorough, and I enjoyed every minute of the class. I learned that the goal with healing touch is to restore energetic alignment to a body's energy system to help people heal themselves.

I was excited for the course, because I was already highly interested in natural healing, metaphysics, and learning more about the body's energy centers, also known as chakras. I also knew the elementary basics of the amazing and mysterious abilities of our bodies to naturally heal. Watching a cut on my finger or a skinned knee heal and transform over time taught me that God ingeniously designed our bodies to know how to self-heal.

I was interested in the effects of emotional stress and trauma on our bodies over time, as well, and with all the reading I was doing, from Louise Hay to Wayne Dyer, in addition to my own sense of understanding, I wanted to know more.

One of the tools used in energy balancing is a pendulum, which we were provided with for the class. I was fascinated with this tool, as we practiced reading the energy of each other's chakras. If an energy chakra was in harmony and balanced, the pendulum would move clockwise, if it wasn't balanced, the pendulum would turn counterclockwise. I learned to clear negative energy and send positive meditative energy if a chakra center was out of balance. I also spent a lot of time practicing using the pendulum and learning to keep my own energy neutral, with my hand still and steady, so the pendulum could clearly pick up on the energy that it was being directed to.

I was so excited to practice on Gary when I got home from the class. I couldn't believe what a positive and powerful life force he had. The pendulum swung like I was twirling it fast, and I wasn't moving my hand. My energy makes the pendulum swing out in a nice easy swing. Gary's energy moves the pendulum like a helicopter rotor blade.

I used the pendulum to read the energy of food, too. Natural foods, like fruits and vegetables, will show positive energy from your pendulum. Processed foods, with sugar, artificial sweeteners, and chemicals, will show you negative energy when holding the pendulum over them.

My three-day Healing Touch course was an eye-opener for me. It ignited something in me, as I connected with energy, our bodies, and the positive ability of our bodies to course correct naturally when we realign our energy.

Of course, I value the Western take on medicine and health, and all that has evolved in that field, to assist people, especially in emergency medicine. I developed my own opinions that both energy medicine and natural healing could be important to anyone's overall health and well-being and highly critical for the prevention of disease and maintaining optimal health.

I must tell you a fun side note about my recent phone conversation with Penny Hanson. I hadn't spoken to her for several years, as she'd moved out of state. The week before we talked on the phone, Penny kept thinking of how she pink flamingoed my yard nearly twenty years earlier, and she couldn't get it out of her head all week. We laughed and talked about how fun life can be when we think about another person and the next thing we know we're talking with them on the phone. We both know Divine Intervention is connecting us.

After September 11, 2001, I made the commitment to myself to start coaching people. My bonus son, Nathan's, wedding was on October 6th of that year, and on that next Monday, October 8th, I called ten people I knew, and they all agreed to allow me to coach them for free. That's how much I wanted to do it. I told them that once I understood the value of what I was providing, I would figure out my fees and start charging accordingly.

I coached small business owners and did personal life coaching for a few friends during those first few weeks. I quickly realized that with my business background, from being a financial advisor for fifteen years, I could provide value to other financial advisors and small business owners. I enjoyed the challenges and commonality that I had with this niche of clients and enjoyed being able to do both business and life mastery coaching for them.

Within three weeks, I could understand and see the value that my coaching provided. I decided to focus on small business clients, and particularly financial advisors, where I could utilize all my experience. From those ten people, I had four paying clients the following month, and by the end of two months, my coaching practice was full.

I knew the importance of learning more, and I wanted to be the best coach I could be, so I enrolled in Coach U, a virtual coach training institution, and graduated three years later. I loved these classes and spending time with the other coach trainers and students.

Thomas Leonard, considered the father of the modern coaching industry by many, had started the coaching movement from a grassroots level. I found it fascinating that he was also a former financial advisor who wanted to coach and impact those he worked with as whole people, not just focusing on their financial goals. I had already realized that when I was a financial advisor, I had been coaching my financial advising clients naturally as part of the services I offered them, and I was interested in all facets of their lives, too.

As I was building my coaching practice, I was curious to see if I could incorporate some of the things that I had read in all the books through the years, as well as my experience with using the pendulum and reading energy.

That's how I named my coaching company, *All Inspired Coaching*. I knew that I wanted the word *inspire* in the name of my company. So one day, I made a list of about thirty different possible names for my company. Some had the word *inspiration* in them, some had the word *inspire*, etc. I typed all these names on a white sheet of paper, listing them one after the other. I took this piece of paper, and I scanned it with my eyes, looking at all the names, and asked, "God, which one is the best name for my coaching company?" Suddenly, *All Inspired* started looking like it was twinkling, and it seemed to lift off the paper and come toward my face.

I thought, "Wow! This is very interesting." I was happy to partner with God's Divine Energy System in this way and loved my company's name.

One of the ways I used my pendulum was to check to see if a potential client was in their office and could take my calls. Those were the days when you paid for long distance calls, and I thought, why waste a call if they're not even in the office so I could talk to them? So, I would take my pendulum and ask if the client was in their office and could take my call. It would move clockwise for yes and counterclockwise for no. It was uncanny how accurate this was, not to mention that I both lowered my business expenses and saved time.

The pendulum has become my favorite energy tool, and I have used it to assist with hiring the best candidates for myself and others, selecting the best options with marketing, and other business and personal decisions. I always tell people when I teach them to use the pendulum, "Divine Energy doesn't lie."

I also realized that my intuitive abilities were amazingly helpful when I was coaching my clients, and I learned to rely on them in almost any situation.

I'd share with clients, "Hey, I'm getting something…," and then I'd share it.

They would almost always resonate with this piece of information and exclaim, "Yes, that's exactly what I was thinking or wondering about. How did you know that?" or "I don't know about that, but it sounds good to me. I'll try it!"

So now, while I rely highly on my intuitive abilities, I like to keep the pendulum handy for confirmation or use it if I'm not picking up anything energetically without it.

I grew up on a farm, and in the old days, and even now, when a well needed to be dug, as every family required water for survival, the simplest and quickest way to know where to dig was by using dowsing or divining forks or rods. These tools have also been commonly used for locating buried metals, ores, gemstones, oil, and other elements. Pendulums are tools to read our Divine Energy System just like dowsing and divining forks/rods energetically locate water and other precious elements underground. When people question my use of the pendulum, I tell them how I learned from my father and both grandfathers, who were all farmers, about energy tools by the time I was eight. So when I was introduced to a pendulum when I was forty-two years old, I was open, willing, and eager to learn how to use this practical and highly accurate tool.

Building a business and living our lives can be difficult and confusing at times, and I am grateful for my Divine abilities and the tools that make the path easier for myself and others.

Have you ever used a pendulum? Make a list of all the ways you could see it assisting you in your life.

CHAPTER 39

Premonition of My Dad's Death

In February of 2003, my dad had a stroke. He'd been a farmer all his life and was used to hard work and living an active life. The stroke paralyzed his esophagus muscles and prevented him from swallowing, drinking, or eating, and made his speech almost indecipherable. He chose to have no medical intervention.

When Mom called with the news, I felt devastated and heartbroken. I learned a person can live between eight and twenty-one days in this condition, and we made plans to go home in a couple of days.

But the next day after I'd talked to Mom, I woke up with a start early that morning. I had a strong feeling and Divine sense that Dad was going to pass very soon. I got up and started packing things for the trip. I told Gary we needed to go down there as soon as possible. He had a couple of things he needed to take care of at the office and said he could be ready to leave at noon. I called my twin sister, Kathleen, and told her about my premonition and that we were leaving at noon. I invited her to drive down to our place and go with us if she could get off work, get packed and down to our place by noon, which she did.

We drove straight to the nursing home and met Mom there. I was in a bit of shock as I walked over to where Dad was sitting. I knew that when a person gets to this point, they are more at peace than their loved ones. I was very emotional and tried not to cry. I was so sad, but I didn't want to waste my time being sad when I was having my last hours with my dad. I wanted to be happy just to be with him, and I was.

At first, I didn't know what to say. I just hugged him. I went to a sink and got a towel and ran cold water on it to place on his forehead, because his forehead seemed hot. I felt useless, but he seemed so happy that we were there. Mom and Gary helped me by softly telling me it was okay to just talk to him and tell him how I felt.

So, I said, "I love you Dad, and I will really miss you." I looked into his eyes and saw the love coming back from him. It was overwhelming love, and I still feel it to this day when I think about our last time together.

I was able to collect myself, and I started talking about good memories that we'd had together. I asked him if he remembered the story of when he put Kathleen and me in the wrong beds one night when we were around two years old. Kathleen was mad the next morning and shook her finger at him; she told him to never put her in the wrong bed again. He remembered, and we all laughed together. We asked him if he would like it if Kathleen and I sang to him, and he nodded yes.

We sang songs we thought he would like. We sang *How Great Thou Art*, *Whispering Hope,* and other favorite hymns. He listened as we sang our favorite childhood Sunday school songs, too. He smiled as he listened and had a spark of light in his eyes. We talked and sang for about three hours that afternoon. It was starting to get dark, and it was time for him to go back to his room and rest.

We talked a few minutes more and then decided we would go back to Mom's and have a quick bite to eat before we left for home. As I walked by Dad's room, I thought I would just peek in and say good-bye one last time if he was awake.

He was awake, but what was happening when I went into his room startled me. He was looking up and to the right, gazing into something that must have been beautiful, because he had a look of wonderment, and almost a smile, on his face. I was struck by what I was witnessing. I did not want to interrupt whatever he was doing, because it seemed like he was having a Divine interaction with something or someone I could not see.

I backed out of his room slowly and quietly. It filled me with such awe, and I was speechless. I shared what I had seen when we got to Mom's house and said that I thought he was communicating with an Angel or a loved one who might be coming to take him Home. His spiritual Home.

I would learn many years later of the Divine phenomena of death bed visitations or DBVs. DBVs are when a person who is close to dying and releasing from their bodies sees a vision of Angels or their deceased loved ones. The dying person can appear to hear messages and sometimes see or call out to their loved ones in Heaven. Family and friends of the dying report this as being very common when their loved ones are in their final stages of dying and transitioning to their spiritual form.

We got back home to Cedar Falls late that night, and Kathleen stayed overnight with us. Around 9 a.m. the next morning, Mom called. She said Dad passed at around 3 a.m.

I was so grateful that I had been given that Divine premonition. I was grateful for the time we were able to share with him before he passed, and seeing him gazing into something beautiful gave me peace.

Another interesting part of this story was that my friend, Barbara Suzanne Morton, called me about an hour after my mom called. When I heard her voice say, "It's Barbara," I asked her, "How did you know?"

She said, "I don't know. I just know that for the last several days, I have been getting a Divine impulse about you, and it was so strong today, I felt I needed to call you."

When I shared with her that my dad had had a stroke and he'd just passed hours earlier, we both cried.

When you have a caring relationship and bond with another person or animal, they are bonded with you through this energy of love for the rest of your life, both in the physical world and in the spiritual world, in Heaven. Barbara was alerted Divinely, felt my emotions through the vibrational energetic frequencies that connected us, and responded.

Some may discount my examples, or yours, of Divine Intervention, as well as the Spiritual Communication System that exists for us to communicate through. But for people who experience Divine Interventions, they feel it in their bodies, have learned to trust these real feelings, and have benefitted by receiving messages of love, protection, and guidance from God and those in the Spiritual Realm, and even from their relationships with the living. Remember, we are spirits in a temporary human body, not bodies in a temporary spirit.

A few months after my dad's death in 2003, my husband came home from work and announced, "We are going to move to a different home. It's going to be a ranch style, it will have an aesthetic appeal, and be very scenic."

Once I heard him say the word "move," I wanted to argue with him right away, as I detested the idea of moving. Besides, I liked the home we were living in at the time, so I didn't take him seriously. Plus, I was just launching my second website, and between that and building my business, I had my hands full. I told him as calmly as I could, "I don't know, hon, this is kind of a bad time for me!"

He was clear that this was going to happen. After we talked again, I asked him how he had come up with this wild idea, one that I wasn't very excited about. He said that this idea just came to him, out of the blue, and he couldn't really explain it, yet he was very clear and certain that it was going to happen.

I now understand that this is exactly what happens when we get a Divine message. It can come out of the blue, you can't always explain it, but you feel clarity and certainty when it arrives. He was getting a very clear Divine message, but we weren't calling it a Divine message at the time. We just referred to it as this *thing* that happened. That's the mistake I think we all make when we aren't clear about where these messages are coming from. While I agree that everyone has the right and free will, given to us by God, to think whatever we want to, it's my belief that Divine Source provides us a Divine relationship with ongoing love, protection, and guidance that is invaluable to us.

Gary called our realtor and asked him to keep an eye out for the "scenic ranch." I just kept rolling my eyes and prayed that he would miraculously forget about it.

We did end up looking at a couple of houses right after that, yet they weren't even close to what Gary had in mind. I was relieved and started to happily forget all about it. Then, a few weeks later, Gary said again that we were going to move to a wonderful scenic ranch house. He just knew it!

A couple of weeks later, our realtor emailed us and said there was a house that he wanted us to look at. He also mentioned that he thought it would sell fast. We got an appointment to look at it the next day. We agreed that we would drive by it, just to see what it looked like before the appointment the next day. When we saw it, we weren't that impressed. Since we'd already made the appointment, we agreed to look at the interior, more out of curiosity than anything else.

That Saturday afternoon, we were the second couple to see it, and as soon as we took four steps into the house, we both stood there with our mouths open in total shock. This home, that didn't look that great from the road, sat high up on a ridge overlooking the Cedar River, and the view took our breath away.

We looked at each other and said at the same time, "This is it; this is our scenic ranch, our new home!"

After looking at the house for forty-five minutes, we began to write an offer. We hadn't prepared to buy that day, yet by Divine nudging, I had put the tape measure in the car, brought it in, and started to measure some of the rooms, just to make sure our furniture would fit into it. As our realtor called the current owner's realtor, letting them know we were writing the offer, we were told they were receiving another offer at the same time. With all the positive energy we could muster, we redid our bid as confidently as possible and went home to let Divine Intention and Energy work for us. We really felt strongly that we were supposed to live in that house and that Gary's premonition about moving was about this house.

A couple of days later, driving back home from Cedar Rapids out of a dark rainstorm, suddenly everything shifted into a lit-up sky. There was a magnificent sunset with the most beautiful and vivid colors and a huge double rainbow. It took both of our breaths away.

We looked at each other and said in unison, "We got the house!"

We were both convinced that the glorious sunset and double rainbow was our Divine sign that we were going to receive the home that had been Divinely messaged to Gary.

Literally ten minutes later, Gary's cellphone rang. You guessed it! It was our realtor telling us that the owners had accepted our offer and that we needed to get home quickly and get the paperwork signed.

Both Gary and I believe that the entire process of us finding this home was Divinely inspired and led.

When in your life have you experienced premonitions that have guided you in helpful ways? Consider keeping a list of your premonitions in your notebook, and remember to date them.

CHAPTER 40

Gary's Healing

Gary and I were having lunch in downtown Cedar Falls when I told him that I probably needed to find a new hair person. I was feeling frustrated with my hair and felt I could use some new feedback.

I happened to be looking out the window, and I said, "There's a salon right across the street. I think I am going to find my new hair person in there."

He said that it was fine for me to go over there, and he would meet me at the car.

I walked into the salon and told the receptionist that I wanted a consultation with someone. I wasn't ready to get my hair cut that day, just wanted some feedback.

She said, "Yes, you can meet with Jessica in a few minutes."

I said, "Okay," and started browsing, looking at all their products in the waiting area.

In a few minutes, Jessica Caughron came to the receptionist's desk and smiled at me. She said, "Come on back."

I liked her energy immediately and hopped up in her chair. I told her that I needed something different with my hair. She ran her fingers through my hair and fluffed it this way and that. I told her I wasn't ready to get my hair cut that day, but I wanted to hear her ideas. I was looking for a professional who was trained to know what my hair could do, as well as what style would look best for my face and fit my lifestyle. I was busy and didn't like taking a huge amount of time with my hair. She looked at my face intently in the mirror and focused on me as if she was in a trance.

Jessica had a quiet confidence about her. I could tell she was an artist. She looked at my face, placed my hair in different positions, and looked at me from various angles.

She told me what she wanted to do with my hair. She showed me a few photos of similar cuts, and I liked them all. She told me that I have fine hair, but lots of it, so she wanted to layer it so it could hold the shape of the cut better. We talked about hair spray, shampoos, and how I could part it in the middle or on the side. She wanted to add highlights too.

I made an appointment for a few days later, and my hair turned out fabulous. The bonus is that she is a wonderful person, and we have developed a great friendship over the years, one that I feel blessed to have. She has been my hair partner for over eighteen years, and the Divine inkling I had that day worked out better than I could have imagined.

In the fall of 2006, I was sitting in my office, and I said out loud, "I am going to meet a quantum healer." I'm not a scientist, but I had been reading and thinking about quantum physics, just the idea of it, not necessarily the practice of it. I knew something was going on with me that had me say that.

After I said it, I accepted it. I really wasn't sure what a quantum healer was, but something about me was manifesting a quantum healer, and I wasn't about to mess with Divine manifesting. Just the sound and idea of it made me really want to meet a quantum healer and learn what they did. I also thought that it would be great to know one and be able to use them as a resource for my own life, as well as for my family, friends, and clients.

Manifesting had become a large part of my life. I was in awe of the Divine process and appreciative of the results. So I accepted the fact that I said what I said, and I knew that at the perfect time, something interesting would happen. Because that's how manifesting works. Then I almost forgot about it, as I got back to focusing on my clients and work schedule.

Gary and I were down in Florida a couple of months later, and we went to Barnes and Noble. We had picked up some books and spent some time browsing.

We were walking towards the door when I told Gary, "Oh, shoot, I was going to see if they had another book I'd been thinking about. I'll be back soon."

I was five feet from the order desk when I heard a woman say, "Hi, I'm here to pick up my book on quantum energetic healing."

I froze and stood at attention. I started remembering that day in my office, when I was twirling around in my chair like a nut and saying, "I am going to meet a quantum healer." This was too good.

I was hoping my voice still worked, as I was coming out of my shocked state, and I ventured forward with, "Um, hi, I hate to interrupt you, but did you say you were picking up a quantum healing book?"

She said, "Yes."

Then I said as I laughed, "I'm pretty sure I manifested you in my office last fall!"

Then she started laughing. She didn't really have time to talk then, as she was taking her mom home, but we exchanged phone numbers. I called her the next day, and I got to know a little more about Sheryl Hensel. We laughed about how we met, and she shared more about what she was doing with her quantum healing work. I was so intrigued that I scheduled an appointment with her for that next week.

When I arrived, she had me lie down on her massage table. She had three very large books open on a credenza. She asked me if I had any pain or health issues that I might want her to address. I really couldn't think of anything in that moment, as I have always been quite healthy. She said that was fine and that she would just do an overall scan and check everything, which sounded perfect to me. She used her fingers for a form of muscle testing called *finger ring testing* to check and verify her informational scan.

After a while, she was done with the overall scan and said that my body was in wonderful shape energetically, which I was happy to hear. I remembered that I have had motion sickness since I was a baby, so I decided to ask her about it. I'd forgotten about it, since it wasn't a huge issue, but it bothered me sometimes when I traveled.

She said, "Okay, let's see."

She said that it was an issue and did an energetic hold where she placed her hands in two areas of my body for a couple of minutes. I just relaxed and closed my eyes.

She said, "Okay, that's now cleared, and you shouldn't have any further trouble with it."

I was amazed when I found that now I can read in a car, which I couldn't before.

Sheryl and I have become wonderful friends, and she is just a phone call away if I need anything.

Gary had a colonoscopy in April of 2010. We were alarmed when the doctor's office called and said they wanted us to go to a renowned medical facility in another state. When we asked what this was all about, they said it was better to talk to the doctors there.

We were frightened. We pushed back and requested another test. They reluctantly agreed and got him in right away for another test. They got the same results the second time, so we agreed to get an appointment at this other clinic, and they scheduled us for two weeks later. Gary was very happy and relieved that he could get an appointment so soon.

I can't remember the name of the diagnosis, but Gary remembers the words were something like "carcinoid neuroendocrine tumors." At the time, I wrote it all down and looked it up on the internet. I was shocked. Anyone who had this disease didn't live more than ten years, and most died between five and ten years after their diagnosis. As I read more about this awful disease, the energy drained out of my body. The gruesome article went on to inform me that they started by taking out the colon, then gradually, over time, took out almost every internal organ, until a person eventually died.

I was in shock and wondered if Gary had looked it up yet. No wonder they didn't want to talk with us and wanted to send us straight to a specialist. I printed out the information and laid it on the kitchen counter, even though I wanted to rip it to shreds. I didn't really want Gary to see it or read it, but I knew he had a right to.

I went back in my office and had a conference with myself. I prayed to God to help Gary, to help us—NOW!!

Because I had been reading about energetic healing, using my intuition with clients, and believed in metaphysics and Divine energy healing, I made a vow that we would do whatever we needed to do. I trusted that God would lead us with Gary's healing process. I made another vow that he was going to be okay.

It all sounded crazy to me, and I decided to call in my friend Sheryl Hensel, the quantum energetics healer who I had met several years before. Through getting to know her and understanding how she helped people, I had great confidence that she could help Gary. We had also become strong friends, and I trusted her with my life and Gary's.

Gary knew her as well and had an appointment with her a few years back for some knee pain. He agreed to meet with her on the phone. It is great to know that many alternative healers and Divine Energy practitioners can do their work over the phone.

We called and put Sheryl on speaker phone. I plugged into my Divine Intuitive and Energetic abilities, as well, and was getting a message that even though something was showing up in his physical body, I sensed that it was something pertaining to emotional issues from his childhood that still hadn't been completely resolved and healed.

She used muscle testing to check in with him, and her information agreed with what I was getting. He needed to heal completely from these incidents in his childhood. She instructed him to write and journal about forgiving the individual involved and then forgiving himself. My sense of things was also that he hadn't completely forgiven himself.

We often blame ourselves when relationships don't work out or bad things happen, especially when we're children. Yet we work at forgiving everyone else and leave ourselves out of the forgiveness equation. Make sure when there is a need to forgive someone that you also forgive yourself, even if you forgive yourself for just being helpless and not able to stop the hurt or pain that you were going through from another person or situation. Unprocessed pain and lack of forgiveness is its own kind of negative energy. And if it's stuck in your belief system, it can show up in your body years later, after the negative energy has worked to corrode and ultimately break down one or several of your physical body's systems.

Sheryl also asked him to write about the gifts and learnings that he had received from this lesson. Then, he was to feel gratitude for complete healing twice a day for the next two weeks, which Gary and I did together. We'd hold hands and thank God for complete healing in the morning and before we went to sleep every night.

Two weeks later, we went to his appointments, and Gary had a slew of medical tests that took four and one-half days. They were extensive, invasive tests. They sent us home for the weekend, and we were to come back that next Monday to learn about the results. In the meantime, we kept positive, and thanked God twice a day for the perfect healing that Gary had received.

Since this was a research hospital, there were about five people in the room when we met with the doctor. There were no introductions made. Everyone seemed nervous as I looked at each of them. The doctor seemed frustrated when we walked in. She was talking to herself and jerking herself back and forth in her chair after she sat down. She'd look at us and stare, then glare back at the computer, which showed all the results of Gary's tests.

Finally, she turned to us and said loudly, "What is going on here? There is nothing on these tests showing up anywhere!"

I slowly raised my hand, wanting her to give me permission to speak, as she appeared upset, and I didn't want to set her off again.

She said, "What?" in a loud and demanding voice, as her eyes now focused on me.

I told her that we had done a Divine Energetic healing two weeks ago, and we had given gratitude to God for complete healing twice a day since then.

She wanted to know who I was. I told her I was Karoleen, Gary's wife. She acted like she was even more frustrated than she had been before. I finally asked if this was good news, that he didn't show any sign of a problem. She was acting so erratically that I couldn't really tell if she thought this was good news or bad.

She loudly said, "We couldn't find anything!" And with that, she and her entourage of three people, who I had a new compassion for, left in a whirl.

The man who was our liaison remained in the room. He was very kind and helpful and told us that, in fact, all the tests had come back negative, which meant they couldn't find anything wrong with Gary. We were so happy and relieved! We knew immediately, as we had for the last two weeks, that he had been Divinely Energetically healed. We were so grateful for Sheryl, as well, for helping us through this scary and difficult time.

For some people, miracles, Divine messages, and healings are seen as impossible, scary, not to be trusted, and even deviant. My experience has proven to me, time after time, they are none of those things.

Gary and I celebrated on our almost five-hour drive home that day by reviewing all the miraculous moments of his healing journey. When we got home, we threw away all the brochures we'd been given and information I had researched and printed from the internet. It all contained information we no longer needed. I gave thanks for all the people out there who work diligently in the healthcare and well-being fields, and we appreciated everything, even the invasive testing that Gary went through to prove he was healthy.

But, without a shadow of doubt in my mind, I gave thanks to our Source and Creator, who is the most powerful and masterful Healer of all. I continue to give the most glory to Him and those who assist in His work.

What miracles of healing have you experienced in your life or that of your loved ones?

Part VIII

Back to the Present— Living the Gifts

CHAPTER 41

Manifesting Trifecta

It was now 2018, and we had just returned home from Florida. I realized I had spent a lot of time organizing my Divine Intervention stories over that previous year, as I turned 60. It felt like a milestone. Taking a complete span through all the miraculous events that had taken place over my lifetime filled me with awe and gratitude.

There was nothing left to do but write the book, but I was tired. I knew enough about energy that I didn't want to force myself to do something just because it was the next step. I decided to trust myself and my own Divine Energy connections and allow the right time to come. I knew I would know when it was supposed to happen, and it wasn't right now.

So I took the pressure off and focused on other joyful and fun parts of my life. I spent time with my friends and family and jumped into gardening that spring. I continued to enjoy the work with my clients; I loved seeing the fantastic results through the simple, yet profound, work we did together.

I believe we are co-creators with the Divine Energy System that was created by our Source, God. I love to manifest using this Divine Energy System, with God as my co-creator, and teach others how to do it, as well.

In the summer of 2019, I was visiting my friend Carol Hellman. She and her sister were planning to go on a hiking trip to the Grand Canyon and wanted to take her son along. It sounded so wonderful to me, as I remembered how beautiful the Grand Canyon was from when we'd visited my other bonus son, Drew, there many years ago.

My friend was rather sad when she told me that the trip was full, and they only had room for her and her sister. It appeared that her son would not get to go.

I looked Carol straight in the eyes, and I said, "Carol, this is a perfect time for you to learn more about manifesting. Are you ready? Would you love to have your son be able to go on this trip with you?"

She looked a little confused, but quickly said "Yes!"

I winked at her, smiled, and said, "Carol, I teach people how to do this for a living. You are in good hands."

I then said, "Okay, you know what you want, which is for all of you to go on this wonderful hiking trip to the Grand Canyon."

I told her to spend the next couple of days feeling how wonderful it would be to have her son on the trip with them. I told her to visualize them hiking, having lunch together while enjoying the amazing views, and imagining them all watching the beautiful sunsets together. I told her to see all the activities they wanted to do together and just allow herself to imagine it, see it, and know that they were going to have the best time, all together. I told her to feel free to talk about it out loud and tell others that she was going to go on this trip, and her son was going to be able to go, too.

Then I said, "Carol, will you do this for the next week, every day, several times each day?"

She was excited about how simple and doable it would be, and she gave me another resounding, "Yes!"

We both laughed, hugged each other, and I said, "Be sure to let me know when your son gets on the list!" and she happily waved, and walked to her car.

That next Wednesday, Carol texted me that her son had been placed on the list. They were all going to get to go. And it only took four days. I winked knowingly at myself and God as I walked by the mirror on my way to my office that morning.

For almost 22 years, I drove my beloved 1998 Toyota Avalon that I called the Silver Bullet. It was a beautiful car, a steel-gray color. My license plate reads NSPIRED, after my company name, All Inspired Coaching. I make friends while driving just because of my license plate, but that's another story.

So, my car's full name was the Silver Bullet Inspired Mobile. It was not only beautiful, but it also had a wonderfully comfortable ride. Simply put, I loved that car. I really didn't want to get a new one, but I felt like it was time.

My husband Gary, who loves to look at new cars, had taken me out once or twice over the last year and a half to look for new cars. I went along to please him and kind of looked at them, but I really didn't get too excited about anything we saw. The truth is, I really don't like to look at cars. I just don't.

In one of my daily conversations with God, I said, "It would be wonderful if this could just be easy. I don't want to go looking for them, I just want to have a new car someday, and I know I will love it."

Gary was going to buy a new Subaru Forester in 2020, so he had all the brochures and had done tons of reading and research on that vehicle. I paid little attention to it all.

One day, he came home with a 2019 Subaru Forester. He just wanted to test drive it; he brought it home for me to see it and asked me if I wanted to drive it back to the dealership. He wanted me to drive it so

I could see if it felt comfortable and if I liked it, as I would, of course, at some time, be needing to drive his car.

So I did. It was raining hard, which I thought was a plus, because I was getting a chance to see if I felt comfortable driving it in not very great conditions. I absolutely loved it. I felt like I was a pilot in an airplane cockpit; I had such an unbelievably wide view. Plus, I was sitting up higher than in my Avalon. As much as I loved my Avalon, I sat low to the ground in it. So I really felt like I was driving a new white stallion.

This is where it started to get dangerous. When I start referring to cars as animals and adding the colors, I know I'm in trouble.

Anyway, we made it back to the dealership and went in, and Cory Hackett, the salesman, asked if we wanted to come in and sit down. I told him I really didn't, as I sat down and got comfortable in the chair. I told him I needed to get home because I was getting hungry.

He laughed. Then he asked me, "Well, how did you like that Forester?"

I said, "I loved it."

He asked, "What did you love about it?"

I said, "Everything. I love the color; I loved driving it; I loved how it felt while I was driving it. I loved how much I could see when I was driving it. I had so much fun. I was driving in torrential rain, and I felt so safe and high up!"

He laughed again. I didn't know why I was making this guy laugh so much.

Then I said, "Why are you asking me all these questions? Because I am not in the market for buying a new vehicle right now."

He stopped laughing and looked serious. He leaned across the desk and said, "The guy that ordered that vehicle you just drove?"

"Yeah," I said, "The White Stallion?"

He continued. "Well, he ordered it five months ago, and in the meantime, he now has a medical issue, and he no longer feels he can buy it."

"Oh," I said, "That's terrible."

He added, "So…"

We both waited.

I spoke first. "Oh…no," I said. "I am *Not* even supposed to be here. I was just driving it over here to get a feel for it."

As I was backpedaling, a strange idea was forming. This is probably the exact car I would have ordered myself. While I hate to look for a car and go through the whole long, annoying process, I had just driven and loved the vehicle that was sitting out there waiting for me—patiently— my White Stallion.

He laughed again, like he had followed my thought process. Now, I started laughing.

I looked at my husband, then at Cory, and said, "There had better be some cookies over there in the showroom, or you may have to buy me a pizza, because if I'm going to take home my White Stallion tonight, I'm going to need some food!"

Then we all laughed.

Anyway, her full name is the White Stallion Inspired Mobile.

The Divine Energy system delivered to me exactly what I wanted and had asked for. While I was in the wave of the whole process, I finally surrendered and allowed it to happen.

I was out doing errands and Christmas shopping for the kids and grandkids at Target. I got mostly stocking stuffers and candy. I felt happy with what I had found, checked out, and drove home.

I discovered when I got home that I had lost one of my favorite earrings. I groaned and started to retrace my steps in my head. I also reached for one of my eight pendulums I had in the house, to help confirm where it most likely was.

I quickly narrowed it down to Target with my intuition and pendulum. It was already around 8:30 p.m., and I was tired. I really didn't want to go back out there again that night. I vowed to head out the next day when I had fresh eyes.

As I drove to Target the next morning, I planned my strategy. I had been in three sections of the store the day before, so I headed to the largest section I had been in. My heart sank as I realized they had probably swept my beloved earring away when they cleaned last night or this morning. But I realigned myself and remembered I had a pretty good idea that the earring was still in the store, and I would find it.

I spent over an hour in that first section, bending down looking, looking, and more looking. I tried to stay out of people's and their cart's way as I hunted. Nothing.

Now this wasn't an expensive earring, it was just one of my favorite ones. Styles change so often in jewelry, so I knew I probably wouldn't find another one, and that was why I was out there. I wanted my earring. And my pendulum had confirmed it was in Target—somewhere.

I went to the second section that I had been in the day before, and again, no luck. I was getting tired and confused but kept telling myself that I knew I was going to find it.

I went to the stocking stuffer section in the front of the store and looked and looked. Nothing. As I stood there, I thought maybe I should go over to the return area and see if they had a lost and found section.

It felt weird, like my feet wouldn't move. I kept thinking I needed to go over to the return section, but again, I wasn't moving. Well, I thought, this is ridiculous. What's wrong with my feet? Why won't they move?

I heard, "*Look down.*"

I looked down at my feet, feeling perplexed. Then I saw something about three inches from my boot. Something sparkly. I bent down and saw my earring.

When I saw my grandchildren, Grace, Olivia, Nolan, and Jamis, later that day, I asked them, "Guess what Grandma found?"

They shook their heads like they didn't have any idea.

I said, "My earring that I lost in Target yesterday."

I love remembering how big their eyes got, and Grace said, "No way!"

I'm always amazed how Divine Intervention helps and guides us. While losing an earring isn't the end of the world or the top priority in anyone's life, experiences like this let you realize that God and his Divine teams are diligent and always helpful, even when the stakes aren't that high. I am humbled when I consider, big or small, we are always being helped and cared for, and our Spiritual Guides are always there for us.

Have you experienced Divine Intervention with small things in your life?

CHAPTER 42

Nathan's Blessings

O n August 10-11, 2020, there was a derecho that lasted 14 hours, primarily across a span of 770 miles across eastern Nebraska, Iowa, Illinois, Wisconsin, and Indiana. It struck with the force of a Category 2 hurricane, but without the usual days of forewarning and chance to prepare. It caused winds of 140 mph, tornadoes, torrential rain, and large hail.

The world didn't even know about it because it came without warning and took the electricity and all forms of communication out with it. It took weeks to get electricity fully restored. My two bonus sons, Nathan and Drew, went to help cut trees and clear debris and said it looked like a war zone. When we finally felt it was safe to go see it, I'd never seen such devastation. Instead of noticing downed trees, it seemed that they were all down, and you would notice maybe one in 1,000 still standing.

Cedar Rapids was one of the towns hardest hit. I was busy collecting nonperishable food and figuring out ways to get it down to Cedar Rapids.

For one trip, our son, Nathan, came over to collect the food and water and planned to head out early the next morning. On the drive down, he realized he forgot to pack the ice to keep the food and drinks cold for the day of work ahead. He hoped others would have some ice when he got there, but they didn't have any, either.

They were trying to figure out where they might get some ice when a truck drove into the driveway, and a young woman yelled, "Hey, do you guys need any ice?"

Nathan could hardly believe it. He called me a day or two later and shared the story of the "Ice Angel" with me, as he knew I was writing a book about Divine Intervention, and he knew I would want to hear his story.

I told him, "It's going in the book!"

Nathan had another Divine Blessing come across his path several months later. We had attended a family member's funeral. Nathan and our grandson, Tristan, were on their way home, and they'd stopped to get gas.

Nathan was on his way into the station to pay for the gas and noticed two women get out of a run-down, junky truck.

One of the women walked toward him and asked, "How are you doing?"

He told her they had just come from a family member's funeral.

She said, as she handed him sage, "We heard you needed a blessing and are bringing you sage for your grieving and saying a prayer for you."

She handed him the sage and shared they were from the Mesquakee, a Native American tribe in Iowa.

With that, they walked away, leaving Nathan and Tristan in sheer amazement. What had just happened? Were these two Native American women Angels from the Spiritual Realm who appeared out of nowhere or were they human angels who had been aware energetically and guided to do a random act of kindness after receiving a Divine message. Either way, it was once again Divine Intervention.

When Nathan and Tristan got in their truck, they took a sacred moment and shared appreciation for this act of kindness. Once they got home, they brought the sage into the house and had another short moment of thanksgiving for being watched over and receiving this blessing.

Divine Blessings come when you least expect them. What Divine Blessings have you experienced? How did you explain them to yourself and others?

CHAPTER 43

Michele's Miracle

August 27, 2020, was a typical Sunday. I was getting ready to make brunch when my friend, Evelyne, called. She rarely called, usually texted, so I wondered if something was up.

Her voice sounded strange. She said, "Michele [Evelyne's daughter] had a brain bleed this morning. They are life-flighting her down to Iowa City right now. All the family are driving down now, as well."

"Oh, no!" I exclaimed, feeling shocked and worried.

I said, "I will start praying and checking in energetically for her."

Evelyne said, "I knew I was supposed to call you. Thank you so much! I will let you know as soon as we know anything."

"Okay—I love you," I said.

"I love you, too."

And with that, we hung up.

I immediately started praying. I asked God for a miracle for Michele. I asked that the doctors would be able to know what to do, for the highest benefit of all.

Then I sat at the kitchen table and cried. Through tears, I shared with Gary what had happened and asked him to pray, too.

Then I went into my office and used the pendulum to check in to see if there was any energetic alignment I needed to do. It said no. I waited.

I made a list of ten of my highly intuitive and Divinely-led friends who I felt would also be willing to pray for my friend's daughter. I sent each of them a text asking them to pray. Throughout the day, I heard from each one with their willingness to pray and send love. I was so grateful.

I checked in with the pendulum every thirty minutes to see if there was anything I was being directed to do. No. It was hard to go through that time with no word from Evelyne.

I was relieved to have several loads of laundry to do, to keep me occupied and moving through the early afternoon. I kept sending Michele love and energetically healing thoughts throughout the day.

At 2:00 p.m., I checked in with my pendulum again. It said it was time to channel Divine Energy and do a Soul Reading for Michele.

I closed my eyes. I focused on her head and brain and allowed myself to relax and focus. I saw a small dark oval, and I began to channel Divine Energy to Michele. There were dark waves flowing around her. I breathed five or six big breaths, blowing the air out with each exhale. I waited. I opened my eyes.

I checked in with the pendulum to find out if there was anything further I was supposed to do. I Divinely sensed Michele was processing love and compassion for herself, from herself and others. With every breath, she was taking in the alignment. I saw that her Soul was clear and in charge. The pendulum directed that there was nothing more that needed to be done, for now.

I texted Evelyne that I channeled Divine Energy to Michele, asked for a miracle, did a Soul Reading on her, and had been Divinely directed to try and talk with Evelyne, if possible. I asked her if it was possible to talk on the phone for a short call.

She texted they had not heard from the doctor yet, and she wanted to wait for that.

I texted her, "Okay."

Then Evelyne called me, so I answered.

"Hi, how's she doing?" I asked.

"The doctor hasn't come out, so I decided to call you."

I shared with her what had happened in the Divine Energetic alignment process and what the Soul Reading had told me.

Then Evelyne asked, "Is she going to be okay?"

I took a big breath. I was feeling uncomfortable with the question, but I told her that from everything I was getting, it looked like she was going to be okay.

Two hours later, Evelyne called me back. The doctor told them she was lucky to be alive, and he didn't know why she was. But he expected her to recover. He stated again that he couldn't explain why she was alive and that he felt their daughter had received a miracle.

This experience shook us all to our core. All I know is that our intention to use Divine Energy matters, and that's what I focus on. It's important to lean into the most powerful healing Divine Energy that exists—from our Creator. And then, all that is left to say is, "Thank You."

Since her miracle, all Michele wants to do is simply help people, and she feels she has found her purpose in life.

Have you ever experienced a miracle that shook you to your core? How did it impact your life?

CHAPTER 44

Messages from Loved Ones

Souls in Heaven come through in readings to help alleviate pain and suffering that their loved ones are going through here on earth. They are eager to come through, to help their loved ones know they are still with them, only in a different form—a form free of their human bodies—their spiritual form.

These souls, now on the Other Side, in Heaven, continue working on spiritually evolving, making progress on their missions, and assisting their loved ones and others on earth.

Souls in Heaven are aware of what is going on in the physical world. They know when their loved ones on earth are in trouble, need comforting and resolution, or a sign that they are close by. They communicate with their loved ones in various ways. Because they are made up of electromagnetic energy that travels at the speed of light, they can instantly manipulate electrical devices such as TVs, radios, cell phones, electrical lights, alarm clocks, etc. At the perfect time for their loved ones, they can turn a TV on or off, play a meaningful song on a radio, send texts, flicker the lights, or make an alarm clock ring when the alarm is turned off—all to let you know they are there.

Your loved ones also communicate through nature and animals. If you have a specific animal, bird, or flower that you associate with your deceased loved ones, they will send an energetic impulse to you through that special flower or bird. If you are open to this form of Spiritual Communication and are aware, you will notice this impulse, see your special sign, and feel their presence. When my mom wants to get my attention, a cardinal will chirp extra loud. For my dad, a blue jay will fly by fast. I enjoy hearing about the special signs that the people I read for have for their deceased loved ones, such as hummingbirds, butterflies, eagles, and more. If this is something you haven't experienced and want to, think of what form of nature makes you think of your deceased loved ones, choose this as your sign for them, and ask them to communicate with you in this way. Then stay open and aware.

But when souls can connect with a medium to deliver a message to their loved one, it gives them a chance to share more in-depth messages and even answer their loved one's questions.

In my work as a medium, with each message I deliver, I feel a sense of bittersweet longing from my clients. They miss their loved ones in their physical form, and that will never change. But a message from your loved ones in Heaven is a special gift. When I received my own messages after my mom died, I was elevated and felt better after that. I still needed to grieve, and I still miss her every day, but I now know that she is close by, and I can communicate with her whenever I want to. I know that she hears me and responds to me Spiritually, in various ways that tell me it's her. I look forward to the next cardinal, the next scent of a cherry pie coming out of the oven when I walk in my kitchen, and the flickering lights in my living room.

Some of the most tender and poignant readings I have delivered have been for mothers and grandmothers from their deceased children or grandchildren. We have a cultural belief that our children or grandchildren shouldn't die before we do. And when they do, it is devastating. The other type of reading that I have done which is also extremely difficult for loved ones left behind is when a death happens by suicide.

I don't usually know what has happened before a reading, but when I do, and it is a deceased child, grandchild, or someone who has crossed over from suicide, I say an extra prayer that I will be able to not only deliver the best reading I am capable of, but that I will also be able to deliver the readings from their loved ones with the most care and compassion possible.

Loved ones left behind on earth often feel guilt that they should have been able to prevent someone from dying, whether it's from a disease, accident, or suicide. Our loved one's spirit comes through to alleviate this guilt, remorse, and pain. They want their loved ones to continue to live joyous lives, knowing they are close by—spiritually here and spiritually available. Spirits in Heaven continue to communicate to me, "*There is no strife, suffering, rejection, or pain here.*"

Loved ones come through with the same personality they had while living on earth. If they were fun, light-hearted, and kind on earth, they will come through to me in that same fun, light-hearted, and kind way to share with their friends or family members.

If our loved ones who are now in Heaven had negative traits or behaviors that hurt their loved ones, they almost always apologize and ask forgiveness of their loved ones during a reading. They do it in a loving and respectful way, not a demanding or forceful way. They are learning better ways in Heaven.

Those souls who died by suicide usually try to help their loved ones focus on their life, not their death. Occasionally they will explain why they ended their life on earth, but they still try to focus on helping their loved ones remember their lives, not their deaths, and they remind their loved ones they are still there, watching over them.

One beautiful young soul who came through for his family with a love of nature and a clear and poetic style of communication said,

"*Don't let my death cloud my life. Even on a cloudy day, when you can't see the sun, the sun is still there.*" His message was powerfully direct about the challenges we all face when our loved ones pass. We can no longer see them in their physical bodies, but they are fully capable of being there for us, watching over us, and they know what is happening in all our lives. Because this soul lived with so much love, joy, and compassion for others, he wanted his family to remember that and focus on his life rather than on how he died.

All the readings I have done from deceased loved ones are powerfully loving and emotional. The love they communicate to and through me for their loved ones is always extremely loving and caring. I am often near tears myself.

While the message from the deceased spirit may be very loving, it may take time for the loved ones left on earth to receive this love, as they may be so distracted and overwhelmed emotionally from the reading itself, especially if this is their first reading or their deceased loved one died recently. If the soul who is deceased was extremely hurtful towards their loved ones during their lifetime, it can take time to process everything. I encourage people to allow themselves to have their feelings, without judgement, as they journey through such tender and difficult experiences.

Through the years, Divine Guidance, along with universal messages from deceased loved ones, have delivered messages about the subject of living and dying for us all to consider:

- *Peace that passes all understanding. Peace is always available. A leaf falls to the ground. A flower blooms for a certain amount of time. Death is also a part of a life on earth, and life on earth has a limited time.*

- *It's important to have understanding about death. We put too much resistance around death. We should allow and accept it. Humans are fearful of death because they don't understand fully that the soul is Divine Energy, and it doesn't die or disappear. Your deceased loved ones are still in your lives—just in a different form.*

- *You can appreciate love in all its forms. Your memories are past experiences of real love. You will always have those. Any positive experience of love with another person or animal is a bond that is never broken.*

- *Our current culture has separated our physical lives from our spiritual lives and has made our physical lives more important. That is a mistake. Spiritual life comes first. Love is more powerful than fear or physical death. We feel loss, but loss leads us to understand more about love.*

- *Everyone is on their own Spiritual path, with their own lessons to learn and their own opportunities to grow and evolve spiritually, both here on earth and in Heaven.*

- *Your time on earth allows for the biggest lessons and evolvement. The most pain leads to the most learning and evolvement.*

- *When you open your heart to greater possibilities of understanding, it leads to compassion, dissolving of resistance, and more appreciation of how much you are loved.*

- *All you take to Heaven with you is Love. You also leave it behind with those you loved in the physical world. Those bonds of love will never break.*

- *Love is always the gift. Life is happening for you not to you, with its lessons and gifts of evolvement. The body isn't first. Divine Soul Energy is first. Length of life doesn't trump how you loved when you lived. Cultural ways do not trump Spiritual ways. Not accepting Spiritual ways causes suffering.*

- *Souls arrive on earth and leave earth at the perfect time, and it is all meant to be celebrated.*

- *Our deceased loved ones want us to keep evolving spiritually, opening our hearts to understanding who we really are, and for us to keep connecting to God and those we love.*

- *In difficult times, ask God to provide the way. Surrender your fears, anger, and hopelessness to God and allow for Spiritual healing. Trust and allow God to give you these miracles—all in God's time and way.*

All these messages are given to inform and remind us that we have been given eternal life. Our soul lives on, growing and expanding—forever. How did these messages make you feel?

CHAPTER 45

Miracle Baby

In December of 2018, we were at close friends, Cory and Stephanie Arensdorf's, home, celebrating their oldest son, Tristan's, eighth birthday with their family. We were also celebrating the news that Stephanie was pregnant with their fourth child. But this wasn't just your typical happy pregnancy news. We were all in a state of awe and wonderment as the details of this miracle began to unfold.

Cory and Stephanie had been blessed with three children: Tristan, Aria, and Austin. They had decided this was the perfect size for their family and felt complete. After their youngest, Austin, was born, Stephanie went through fallopian tubal ligation surgery. They were content with their beautiful and growing family. Cory and Stephanie began to dream and talk about outings and vacations that they felt like they could start planning, as Austin was growing out of the baby stage and everything that can tie you down with very young children.

But this is where their story starts getting interesting. At the time of Stephanie's pregnancy with Austin, Cory's Mom, Kathy Arensdorf, had a dream that there were going to be two babies, one boy and one girl. Grandma Kathy had experienced dreams about all of Cory and Stephanie's children before they were born, and they had all proven true. Yet when Austin was born and there was only one baby, Kathy still felt there was a baby girl coming. Even after Stephanie's tubal ligation surgery, when Kathy thought of her dream, she still felt there was a baby girl in the works. Her intuitive feelings were strong.

When Stephanie was first pregnant with their oldest child, Tristan, Kathy had a dream with her own dad in it. He was holding a baby, and he told Kathy, "*I got to hold him first.*" With the Divine message from this dream, she learned from her dad's spirit that the baby would be a boy.

When Grandma Kathy found out Stephanie was pregnant with second-born Aria, she'd had another dream of a baby and knew it would be a little girl.

Stephanie's Mom, Marilyn Yoder, also played an important role in this miracle baby's story. Grandma Marilyn started crying at night because she wanted another grandbaby. She asked God for another grandchild. When Austin became a toddler, with her strong desire for another grandbaby, Grandma Marilyn began many conversations and sent many prayers to God with her sacred request.

Stephanie had just stopped breastfeeding Austin three months earlier, and her periods were starting again, and they were regular. Stephanie noticed she was late and didn't feel like eating. She also felt like she had with her other pregnancies. And with Stephanie being a foodie and loving food, this seemed like it could only mean one thing. Could it be? Could she be pregnant? She called Cory and asked him to pick up a couple of pregnancy tests on his way home from work. He went right to joy and excitement. Stephanie tried to calm him down. She didn't want to get his hopes up, as she had been warned that with her surgery, sometimes a tubal pregnancy can happen, and the baby isn't able to develop.

When Cory got home, Stephanie did the pregnancy test. It showed bright pink immediately. There was no waiting time of a couple minutes or even seconds. It was instant. The real deal. A baby.

Wanting confirmation, Stephanie took a second pregnancy test the next day. Instant bright pink again. She scheduled an ultrasound test to find out if it was in her fallopian tube. Nope. This was going to happen. It was real.

When Grandma Marilyn found out Stephanie was indeed pregnant, she was ecstatic and so grateful to God for this miracle. She told me, "God heard me crying for another grandchild!"

When Grandma Kathy found out, she not only felt joy and excitement, but she also felt relieved that her Divine intuitive feelings, knowings, and dreams had again been correct.

When Stephanie delivered her sweet miracle baby girl on May 1, 2019, they talked about what they wanted to name her. While she and Cory discussed many names, it seemed perfectly fitting when they shared the news that she would be named Mira, for the little miracle that she was to all of us.

When I think of a miracle, I always think of this story about Mira. The power of your dreams and desires is extremely potent, as shown by Mira's two grandmothers. Grandmothers Marilyn and Kathy trusted their prayers to God and their Divine dreams from God about Mira coming.

We live in a Divine Energy System of God's creation. Whatever we dream and pray about has a vibrational and magnetic force and frequency of Divine intention. Even though the odds may be against what you dream and desire, never discount how being steadfast, as you partner and co-create with the most powerful loving energy of our Creator, can bring you miracle after miracle.

Have you manifested miracles in your life? What miracles would you like to co-create?

Epilogue

I had no idea that I would learn so much more about Divine Intervention through writing *Opening to Divine Intervention*. At first, I just wanted to share my stories. Then I started thinking a lot about what I wanted to share with you besides the stories. The Fifteen Types of Divine Intervention and the Five-Step ACUTE System for Spiritual Communication came from my desire to assist you with accepting, claiming, and expanding your own intuitive abilities. I also hope you will connect my stories with your stories and allow your memories to awaken you to the Divine Intervention moments you have experienced.

It was also important to me that you understand that while these Divine Interventions happened throughout my life, my turning point moments at the age of 54 jolted me awake to a higher level of perception and an ongoing array of Divine Intervention experiences that expanded my spiritual awareness and abilities. Eventually, I realized that my entire life had been Spiritually guided, and I knew not only what the book would be *about*, but I also knew that I needed to take myself, and you with me, back through my early years to get the *fully connected* story. And in doing so, I wanted to invite you to investigate and see more of your own *Spiritually Connected* life.

At various times while writing this book, I have wondered how I would end it. I really didn't know, yet I felt that the ending would be very important. I was filled with questions but had no answers.

As I have done throughout my life, I continued to do several things when I wanted to find answers. First, I asked God for help. I prayed for help with the ending of this book. Second, I trusted God that when I was ready to have the answers about the ending, they would be Divinely revealed to me. And third, I surrendered my questions fully to my Divine Co-Creator/God. I held the space for Divine answers to come.

On May 23, 2022, ten years and one day since the passing of my mom, I was surrounded by my index cards that were filled with the notes, thoughts, and ideas I'd written down over the last couple of years that seemed important for the book. Looking through them felt more overwhelming than helpful, but this day, I felt compelled to go through a large stack of them.

I came to a card that was almost blank. That was unusual, as most of my index cards have a lot of writing on them. But I paused when I came to this card. It had only "Revelations" written on it. I felt something stir in me.

According to Google, a *revelation* is "a surprising and previously unknown fact, especially one that is made known in a dramatic way." It can also mean, "the divine or supernatural disclosure to humans of something relating to human existence or the world."

Revelations is also the name of the last chapter in the New Testament of the Bible. After spending some time reading Revelations, I started wondering about the ending of the Bible's Old Testament. I picked up my Bible again and looked for the last book in the Old Testament and came to Malachi. *Malachi* means "my messenger." I learned that Malachi was God's messenger to the Jews following the rebuilding of the temple.

I also learned that the people were not relating to God in the way He intended; they weren't putting their spiritual relationship first and honoring God for all that He'd given to them. Malachi reminded people that their relationship with God was the most important part of their lives. He wanted them to know that their desire to love and honor their Creator and keep pure intentions of being in close relationship with God was what mattered. It mattered more than the Temple, and it mattered more than religion.

In Malachi, I learned that those who wanted to honor God wrote words of remembrance to show their reverence and respect—and God heard them.

In *Opening to Divine Intervention*, I have shared some of my *remembrances* of how God has loved, protected, and guided me through so many times of my life—the joys, heartaches, best, worst, and lost days, too.

I was filled with quiet excitement and reverence for God as I was led to writing the ending of this book. *Opening to Divine Intervention* is my *Book of Remembrance*.

I encourage you, as you read this book, to make a note in the Table of Contents of what stories were most significant to you, so you can easily find them again. I hope you write down your own stories of Divine Intervention. Writing down the most important Divine moments of our lives helps us to remember them, and then we can review them anytime we want to.

You might even want to create your own Divine Intervention Circles, where you invite your friends to join you and share your Divine Intervention stories, big and small, with each other. Feel free to use this book, including the questions for reflection in the chapters and the Fifteen Types of Divine Intervention list, as a reference to guide you.

People learn best from stories. I hope my Divine Intervention stories will teach you as they have taught me. Whenever I'm down, I like to think of my stories. They fill me with such joy, love, and peace. I hope they do the same for you.

With every ending, there is a new beginning. And like in death, there really is no ending—but always a beautiful new beginning.

And with this new beginning, I have come to some conclusions:

- With so many Divine Intervention experiences, I now trust my ability to communicate spiritually, both to send and receive messages.

- I choose to continue to listen, be aware, respect, trust, and enjoy my Spiritual Communication System, because it is working for me, feels right, Divine, and good.

- I am okay with others' choices and respect their right to decide for themselves on this subject. We all have free will. And everyone's relationship with God is personal and unique, as it should be. It's also important to remember not everyone wants to share their Divine experiences. When I was growing up, that seemed to be the case, because I didn't hear too many people talking openly about their Divine experiences.

- Because it became my calling, I choose to assist others if they want to activate, strengthen, and expand their abilities to use their own Spiritual Communication System.

- God and His Spiritual Realm sent me many gifts at many times in many ways; they sent love, protection, and guidance to me. I received and appreciated these gifts that were sent with such love. I was led to discover, claim, expand, and strengthen my Spiritual Communication (our original language) abilities. As I did, I came to trust these messages even more and began to enjoy and appreciate the amazing Divine Partnership and communication system we have been given. My wish for you is that you find these things in your own life, too.

So now what? What's next?

I'm learning not to put any limits on my abilities and trust that by saying yes to my Creator, I don't have to be in control of what I'm able to do. I just need to stay open, aware, sense what I am resonating with, and enjoy it all. I look forward to what is in my life now and what's ahead, as more souls wake up to their Divine Partnership and realize their full access to Spiritual Communication.

My friend, Evelyne, told me one day, "You're like a disciple for God."

I told her I did feel like an *ambassador* for God and a *spiritual activist*.

My favorite question to ask people is still, "How is God working in your life right now?"

And I can't wait for all the answers I will receive. I encourage you to share your own Divine Intervention stories and ask yourself how God is working in your life.

So many times, I have been touched by the love of our Creator through these amazing Divine experiences. I have thanked God so many times. Every time the moments and messages come, I have said to God, "That was so beautiful. If it all stopped now, it would be more than enough."

Even though I don't want them to stop coming, I feel so grateful for all that I have already received.

My invitation to you is to join me in staying aware of our present-day life of miracles and Divine Intervention. I was Divinely told that this was another of the important reasons for me to write this book. Once you experience Divine Intervention for yourself, it can change you forever. It changed me forever in the beautiful ways that I have shared.

Be an open learner. If you can be open and willing to learn from Divine Guidance, your life can make more sense and have more meaning. Through my stories of my experiences, I hope you will learn how to manifest, activate your Divine Partnership, and learn the simple steps to perceiving and receiving your Divine messages. I also invite you to follow the Five-Step ACUTE System and re-establish your connection with your already-in-place, intact Divine Communication System. When we deny Spiritual Communication for ourselves, we stop our glorious awareness and keep Divine Guidance away from our lives. When you are in over your head with troubles, start praying and asking for help from your Spiritual team. Your Spiritual team is made up of miracle workers, and they will help you. Let Divine Intervention work for you.

Now, with *Opening to Divine Intervention* completed, I feel that it will go places that will surprise and delight me. It will have a life of its own as I set it free to do what it was created to do and touch lives in ways that I may never know. I look forward to meeting others who are excited about their Divine Intervention experiences and to seeing who might want assistance in speeding their progress of activating and expanding their Spiritual Communication abilities through mentoring and coaching. I have an open heart and trust God to assist me on my Spiritual path wherever it leads. And I wish the same for you, for the Highest Benefit of All.

Whatever happens, you know it's going to be good—because it is God.

Call to Action

Are you ready to learn more
about developing
your Intuitive Abilities?

Get your complimentary
Intuition Development Assessment at:
KaroleenFober.com

Acknowledgments

There are so many people both here and in Heaven who I want to thank. You each made a difference in my life, and together we created bonds of love and appreciation that will never be broken.

I'd like to give an appreciative thank you to all my clients and everyone else in my life for their trust in me through the years to provide them with messages of Divine Guidance for the Highest Benefit of All. Whether it was assisting you in choosing your best options and strategies to expand or streamline your business and life, leverage your gifts, notice your energy blocks to get you unstuck so you could move forward, or provide comfort and resolution after the loss of your loved ones, it's been the honor of my life to serve you all.

A big ovation goes to Capucia Publishing, under the vision and guidance of Christine Kloser, Carrie Jareed, and their entire team. Karen Burton, Director of Editing, and my editor, Susan Bruck, helped bring this book to its highest form.

Ethel Morrow Harryman, my mom—You taught me how to pray, love, and rely on God, to happily make lemonade out of lemons, and modeled doing your best, all with great generosity for others and a song in your heart. How fortunate for me that you were a highly evolved soul. With your unassuming purity and the perfect combination of kindness, fun, and zest for life, you modeled Heaven on earth for all. I carry you with me in my heart everywhere I go, and your life is my compass. With your departure to Heaven, our love bond opened me up for my next level of understanding and expansion in Spiritual Communication and my soul's mission. What a God and Mom-send, as I don't think I could live without knowing you will always be in my life.

Bruce L. Harryman, Jr., my dad—You taught me about respect and conservation of our earth, the weather, and about the life of a farmer and taking care of property and animals. You also taught me to respect myself even when doing that put me at odds with you or others. Both you and Mom taught me responsibility, perseverance, and that it was good to get up and take care of what had to be done every day. You seemed to be the one who had to teach me the hardest lessons, but you knew I had to be strong, be able to stand up for myself, navigate for myself in the life ahead of me, and know right from wrong. Your best made my life better, and I learned forgiveness, compassion, and to strive to stay in my own loving alignment when fear tries to dominate. I think you were highly sensitive like me. There were moments of unconditional connection with you where I felt I was totally appreciated, understood, and seen in a way that I've never felt from anyone else. Now, with you only a few seconds away and always available in Heaven, our disappointments healed, we have what we both always longed for, a close and loving relationship.

Lawrence (Larry), Colleen (CoCo), Lois, and Kathleen, my precious siblings—Thank you for all the fun, love, and joy we got to share together. You are each such beautiful and innocent souls. You have always been by my side when I needed you. Thank you for always inspiring me and helping me through life's ups and downs. You are all my heroes. I look forward to more wonderful times together with all your spouses, too, whom I adore.

And now for my grandparents—You were all so wonderful and significant to me, I could write an entire book about each one of you. Emily Stewart Patterson Morrow and James A. Morrow, my maternal grandparents—having you only ten miles away and living on your own beautiful farm was this grandchild's dream come true. Dora Belle Wolfe Harryman and Bruce L. Harryman, Sr.—my paternal grandparents—forty miles away was close enough for me to get in on the action of Grandpa's whirlwind work and business energy, with

Grandma hanging on for dear life with her famous wit and wisdom, one-liners that always left me inspired, laughing my head off (even now), or wondering deeply about what she had just said. I always felt safe, loved, cared for, pampered, and special in your presence. How blessed I was to spend so much time with all of you—Grandma Morrow would visit us almost every Saturday afternoon with freshly baked dinner rolls and chocolate chip cookies in her basket. Grandma and Grandpa Harryman arrived on Sundays for dinner and a visit with books and the best oatmeal raisin cookies I've ever had. Of course, the best times were when we could go and stay overnight with you and get the royal grandparent doting that filled my life with the best experiences and memories ever. My own times as a grandparent have been magical for me, and I feel so blessed to have had the four of you to show me how it was done.

Emmett Morrow, my great-uncle (No biological relation to Mom's Morrow side. He married Grandma Dora Belle Harryman's sister.)— Knowing that you helped build the Golden Gate bridge in San Francisco impressed me right away. But when you moved back to your family homestead when I was a kid and became Dad's right arm to help on our farm was when I got to experience your human angel qualities, as you performed manual labor in your 70s like a teenager. But your connection and understanding with my dad seemed to ease the parts of his heart that had been broken. You walked in the world with the peace that passes all understanding, were a friend to all, and I watched you perform miracle after miracle.

Anna and Delber Plowman, our neighbors and friends that lived a mile away when I was growing up—You seemed like another set of grandparents to me and always had treats ready and waiting for our weekly visits. I know you were primarily Mom's friends, but I benefitted from your help on Sundays, always taking us to Sunday school and church and taking us home if Mom couldn't make it because of extra chores she needed to take care of. Thanks, too, for taking Mom to the hospital before Kathleen and I were born. You were some of our first Godsends who continued to bless us all during my growing-up years.

Barbara Wilson Hodge—You were the best babysitter in the world, and I was so blessed to be taken care of by you and Stanley. I'm sending hugs up to you and Stanley in Heaven.

Mr. Camille Price, my high school creative writing teacher—I'm pretty sure that this book would not exist unless you had written "qualities of a good writer" in red on one of my writing assignments when I was fifteen years old. I don't remember having a lot of confidence in my writing; I just knew I liked doing it. Your response to me made me feel good about what I had done, and that has stayed with me all these years. You had high respect and expectations for everyone in your classroom. You made me feel like I had somehow reached those expectations, even though I'm not sure I always did. Thank you for your generosity and writing the words of potential you envisioned. Because of you, I try to pass on encouragement for others' efforts when I notice good things happening.

Gary Fober—You're simply the best. I was convinced I wouldn't find what I was looking for. But then, when I surrendered it all and trusted God to figure it out, you appeared. What a wonderful life we have created together, with God as our leader and provider. And while we are husband and wife, we are also spiritual partners. I love our commitment to spiritual growth and evolvement as we look at each new day as an adventure and opportunity. Honey, I know the best is yet to come!

Aimee, Ernie, Nathan, Candace, Drew, and Renee—I can't imagine my life without all of you. Thank you for all the priceless fun and joyful adventures we've all been on together. Let all the love we have for each other continue to grace our lives forever.

Emma Louise Traugh, Keeley Rae Fober, Ethan Charles Traugh, Tristan Michael Fober, Grace Louise Fober, Olivia Leigh Fober, Nolan Hughes Fober, Jamis John Fober—What a privilege it has been to be your Gram. I have loved every minute of watching each of you grow and develop into such wonderful, interesting, and loving people. I am so proud of you and will always be your greatest cheerleader. Our bonds of love will last forever, so I will always be close by if you need me. I love you to the beach and back.

Stephanie, Cory, Tristan, Aria, Austin, and Mira Arensdorf—You have enriched my life with your love, thoughtfulness, and care, and we are forever connected. It will be fun and exciting to experience all the new adventures ahead.

Danielle McCulley and Blaiklee Schatz—What pure pleasure it is having both of you in my life. You are both very bright stars of love and light. You inspire me as you lead your lives with your hearts.

Carol Hellman—You are the most wonderful friend a girl could ever hope for. I have cherished every moment of our friendship through the years, and I look forward to more great times together. Life is so much better with you in it.

Evelyne Emma Berta Marianne Cavet Jennings—I promised you I would put your most beautiful name in my book, and it matches the beauty of the woman you are—inside and out. I love our story of how we met at the Festival of Trees, a story of manifesting at its best. I look forward to my life with my dear soul sister and friend and can feel the excitement in the air for our adventures ahead!

Connie and Sue Nichols—Thank you for being such wonderful friends and neighbors through the years. Our bond of love and friendship is so special to me, and you've both made such a difference in my life. I love you both.

Dan and Becky Corbin—How blessed we are to have you both in our lives. There could not be more caring friends and neighbors than you.

Joyce Barbatti—What can I say, dear friend? You have been a huge light and delight in my world for so many years. If there is one person who has inspired me to write this book, it's been you. You and I have been talking about Divine Intervention since we met.

Sharing our Divine Intervention stories and discussing how God has been working in our lives has been so meaningful to me and is the foundation of our friendship. Your calling to open TJ's Christian Bookstore and watching it all unfold has been really beautiful. I am so grateful for you and how this new venture serves people, wherever they are in their faith journey. Knowing you are enhancing so many lives fills me with joy.

Russell Jarvis—Thanks for being such a great friend to me since seventh grade. I hope you know how valuable your friendship has been to me, especially during these last ten years since my mom got sick and passed, and through my Spiritual Communication expansion. You were a rock of stability and support as I journeyed and found my way. Thank you from the bottom of my heart, dear friend.

Guelda Cronk—You were such a wonderful friend of Mom's. When she became sick and went to the hospital, you were there for me in so many ways. We are kindred spirits. You let me lean into your strength and understanding, and I will never forget your kindness. You touched the lives of three generations of my maternal family and blessed us all.

Christie Daugherty—I'm so glad we connected ten years ago. To know that you are now living in the home where my mom and grandma lived and where I spent so many happy times makes my heart joyful and at peace. We created a beautiful connecting bond, and I'm so happy to know you. You are a new and delightful friend and a strong and shining light in your community. Shine on!

My Book Writing Group members—How wonderful to journey with you seven brave and beautiful women on our book writing quest. I fell in love with each of you through your open hearts, beautiful faces and souls, and your books' intentions. You each showed up authentically and shared your wisdom and discoveries of your soon-to-be gifts to the world. That allowed all of us to receive inspiration for our own books. Your love and support have lifted me and this book up with new awareness and energy each time we gathered. So glad we all resonated with and said "yes" to Christine Kloser's invitation and magical leadership. I adore each of you, and I can't wait to read your books! I will never forget the ride we all took together and how you all made such a rich impact in my life.

Deblyn Russell—I loved your entrance into my life and the times we connected. Your down-home energy was always inviting, accepting, and beautifully combined with your unending creativity and beautiful offerings. You are inspirational and a blessing to this world.

Carol Mauer—You were my first welcome into expanding my Spiritual Communication and accepting myself as a medium. You are a beautiful friend and mentor to me. You saw and spoke my gifts so I could accept and claim them and step into my Soul's new mission. Your walk in the world helped make mine possible. The reason I now mentor and coach other Light Workers is because of your great gift of kindness and encouragement to me. I pass the baton because of you.

Maria Peth—I love your deep and insightful wisdom, and I'm so happy for our connection. Your presence and gifts serve so many so radiantly.

Sandy Praska—What a delightful light you are. You had me at "hello." Your gifts as a Light Worker are many, and your friendship has touched me profoundly.

Kate Thoma—You are a massage therapist extraordinaire. My healing process was enhanced and supported by you for so many years. You are my Soul Sister forever. Thank you. Thank you.

Laurie Hazel—I love the unassuming brilliance of how you deliver your gifts and walk in the world. You've become a dear and trusted confidant and friend.

Dee Loecher—Every time we've connected, I get to see more of your many-faceted brilliance. Like a diamond, you shine brilliantly in many ways and on so many levels. Our conversations are esoterically beautiful as we cut to the chase so quickly and easily. Like a professional barrel racer, you can turn on a dime and leap into the next level of evolvement. Girl, you are an experience to behold, and I love the way you think and talk! I am thrilled to be your friend.

Joan Johnston—Dear Joan, I just love you! I've never met anyone who can move so many mountains so easily and be so humble about it. You're on my A-team list forever. You're always there and responsive in the most wonderfully accepting ways. Walking in the world is so much better because you're in it.

Barbara Suzanne Morton—I am humbled when I think of you and the huge impact you've made in my life. You were able to reflect to me exactly who I was, and I wanted to see what you saw! You cleared the paths for so many so that we could continue bravely on. Your gifts to me were many, and I received them all fully. Your creative Namaste time and space provided fertile ground for my growth, and I will be forever in a place of appreciation for your steadfast confidence and trust in me. You always maintained there was plenty of room for all the twinkling stars to shine as brightly as possible.

Janine Ambrose, PhD—Your unassuming finesse in so many areas of creativity—music, life experience, friendship, spiritual communication, therapeutic counseling, visioning, and business—is inspiring to behold. Then I discovered your sprinkling of ease and fun matched my own exuberance for creating fun and enjoyment, and I knew we were a good match. I love that we always meet in the place of "Yes!" Thank you for hitting the *Happy Ball* of life back to me so expertly.

Penny Hanson—I'm so happy you are in my life. Learning about Healing Touch and how to use the pendulum changed my life. Your gifts of being a great teacher and angel to the healing arts opened hearts, minds, and hands to join and serve. I salute you.

Renee Wilke—Thank you for your help in reconnecting me with some of our Soul Sisters from the Namaste years. I appreciated it greatly. Your artistic gifts always take my breath away, and I can't wait to see your mosaic guitars.

Jessica Caughron—My hair guru and highly intuitive friend. You are a treasure in my life in so many ways. I simply love you.

Sheryl Hensel—I love our manifesting story of how we met. You have been a true Soul Sister to me in every way. You are one of my favorite people of all time, and I'm so blessed by your presence and friendship in my life.

Cory Hackett—Thank you for being a part of my book. Buying my car was a truly magical experience, and I appreciate your help and expertise.

Michele Wetzel—You are a warm and sweet soul, and I'm so glad I know you. Your emergency brought us together, but it is our bond of love that connects us forever. I love you.

Bonnie Winninger—You are such a loving, delightful, and talented soul, and I'm so glad we were brought together. I look forward to more times together, beautiful Soul Sister.

Kathy Arensdorf—It was so wonderful meeting you through your amazing son, Cory, and daughter-in-law, Stephanie, and experiencing our growing friendship. I love that the miracle stories keep happening, and I look forward to more great times together.

Marilyn Yoder—You are such a warm and delightful person, and I always enjoy your company. Through your darling daughter, Stephanie, I am so pleased to be gifted with your friendship.

Bonnie Merryfield—You got the fire burning when you wrote your amazing book several years ago. Thank you for inspiring me, being a wonderful and supportive friend, and leading the way.

Susan and Don Mendenhall—Thank you for your dear friendship through the years and providing your love, amazing insight, and support to me. I love your flow of beautiful creative endeavors. You both inspire me.

Angie Reuter—I always look forward to seeing you and enjoy our conversations. Your life has been awe-inspiring to me, and I'm blessed we are friends.

Terri McWilliams—We met right after college during our first year of teaching, and I loved that we became fast friends right away. You are a supreme uplifter, and I love every minute we get to spend together. Thank you for being my forever friend.

John and Sonia Stookesberry—What a full circle of Divine Intervention experiences we had together. I loved getting to know you both because of your connection to Mom and through John's help with selling her house. I love how God is always in the mix and creating miracles, big and small, to assist us. I know Mom is smiling down on us, too.

Jay Stookesberry—How wonderful to learn about you all grown up and with your multiple musical talents being utilized in so many areas. I can understand now why Mom was always raving about you. You have made her proud, lifted her legacy, and begun your own. What a beautiful life you are living, bringing music to so many.

Marlys Staudt—Thank you for being my long-time friend who knows me so well. You are a touchstone for me, and I love how we have always focused on our spiritual paths. I love you.

Dan and Kay Henderson—Thank you to both of you for always being there for Gary and me. We miss you as our neighbors, but you will always be dear friends and just a phone call away.

Pam Gibson—Hugs to you, my dear friend. I've loved our time together. It was such a highlight of my year to spend time with you on your Light Worker journey, and I always looked forward to our conversations. So proud of you! Shine on!

Deb Schnadt—I feel so blessed to have met you, and I know that God put us together that day because of how we resonated with each other's souls and connected for life. I love your fire and spunkiness and how you don't hold back. We had a pivotal phone conversation back on 2-18-2020 about this book. I was feeling doubt, and you spoke with clarity and power of its truth and light. Thank you, dear friend, for your love and support.

Kathy Hendershot-Hurd—Thank you for always having great vision and giving me your best. Your feedback is always spot on, and I am so grateful for your expertise and care. You are the best!

Kim Brown—You were one of the first people I told I was planning to write a book. I was so grateful for your uplifting response. You told me to hurry up and write it because you couldn't wait to read it! Thank you for your own Divine gifts, your encouragement, and for cheering me on!

Marci Shimoff, Curt Swarm, Cindy Anne Mathers, Laurie Hazel, Kate Wirtjes, Chequita McCullough, Anela Arcari, and Erin Moroney LaBelle—Each of your lights shine so brightly in the world as you inspire others with your gifts. I am blessed by your friendship and generosity.

Keri Miller—Thank you for landing back in my life at the perfect time! Your talents and expertise blow me away and I look forward to our journey ahead!

Thank you to Sue B., Pat, Billie, Dana, Theresa, Linda, and all the others who were part of this book. I will always be grateful.

To God and my spiritual team—Thank you for all the love, protection, and guidance you have provided for the Highest Benefit of All.

And to you, the reader, I appreciate this Divine journey we are on together.

Appendix 1

15 Types of Divine Intervention (DI)

1. **Miracles**: All forms of DI can be referred to as miracles. This word is used by the general population to describe an experience that cannot be explained from the point of view of the physical world that we live in, so the only other option is to define its occurrence as caused by God / the Spiritual Realm / Heaven.

2. **Divine Readings from Others**: Where someone reads the energetic frequency of your Soul. I call these Soul Readings. Divine wisdom, predictions, and other helpful messages come through.

3. **Self-Soul Readings**: This is where you read your own energy frequency and tap into your own Divine Wisdom.

4. **Divine Pivotal Moments**: Where a Divine Spiritual message comes through, and it is a life-changing moment for you, where you have a major awakening about a situation or a directional change in your life.

5. **Divine Lessons**: This is where your Divine experience teaches you something significant; you learn a life lesson on a deep level, and you incorporate it into your life as you move forward.

6. **Divine Asking, Praying, Manifesting**: This is where you consciously ask God / Holy Spirit / Divine Guidance / Higher Power for what you want. You are connecting with the energetic frequencies of the Divine Spiritual Realm.

7. **Dreams and Premonitions**: At night, when our brains are between Alpha waves, which is the relaxed state, and Theta waves, which is our dream state, we can receive communication from Divine Guidance and our loved ones' spirits through dreams. Almost everyone has experienced this before. You might also experience premonitions during your waking day, which is when you are in the Beta-wave brain state. Premonitions are usually messages of warning. Whether positive or negative, they are always helpful. They alert you to information so that you might alter the course of your day or be extra careful and aware of your surroundings.

8. **Direct Divine Communication**: You get a message that you can see, hear, know, or feel. You sense it, understanding the Divine Energetic Communication that is being sent through the Spiritual Realm. You may also be able to smell scents or taste something if it's important to the message.

9. **Natural Healings/Energetic Body Alignments**: Some refer to these as Medical Miracles. This is where you receive Divine Healing from the Divine Energy Source that is directed to you by yourself or a practitioner. There are many modalities of natural healing, such as Healing Touch, Reiki, Reflexology, and others.

10. **Angels: Human, Heavenly, and Animals**: This is where Angels interact from Heaven/the Other Side/the Spiritual Realm to help with a situation in our physical world. Humans in the physical world may feel the impulse to provide help to others and not know why. They may feel an impulse to help someone they don't know that feels like a "Godsend" or a miracle to the receiver. Also, Angels from Heaven can change into human form and appear seemingly out of nowhere, and it's impossible to explain how they appeared. They are usually not seen arriving or leaving. Animals, in physical or spiritual form, can also aid humans through their abilities to connect with us with help from Heaven.

11. **Divine Creations**: These Interventions include all forms of creativity where the idea for something, such as a poem, a song, or a new solution to a problem, appears out of the blue or sometimes just after you wake up. You feel like it has been Divinely given to you.

12. **Near-Death Experiences (NDEs) and Death Bed Visions and Visitations (DBVs)**: NDEs are when a person's body dies, and their soul leaves the body and travels to the Spiritual Realm/ Heaven. Many times, they see their deceased loved ones, follow the Light, and experience Heaven in some form. Then they are usually given a choice of whether to return to their bodies or remain in Heaven. DBVs occur when a person is close to dying and releasing from their bodies. They may see a vision of Angels or loved ones, hear messages, and see and call out to their loved ones who have passed. Many family members or friends have reported witnessing their dying loved one experiencing this access to the Spiritual Realm.

13. **Mediumship**: This is where you receive messages from deceased loved ones through your own abilities or someone else's. These Divinely communicated messages provide love, comfort, and resolution. Psychometry is reading the energy of a deceased loved one's spirit by holding an object that the deceased spirit is connected to, such as a piece of jewelry, watch, or clothing item, etc. The object can be something they used, wore, owned, or gave as a gift.

14. **Divine Journaling**: This is where a person connects to the Divine Source and can receive helpful messages of Divine Guidance or from deceased loved ones through writing.

15. **Natural Phenomena**: This is where a Divine Intervention is experienced through the natural world: through weather changes, messages in the sky, found items like coins, a physical machine stopping or starting, items being moved in your home, light bulbs flickering, being in an accident and escaping unharmed or with few injuries, and many other experiences that Divine Guidance/God or deceased loved ones use to get messages to you or to protect you.

Appendix 2

Five-Step ACUTE System for Spiritual Communication
(Refer to Chapter 6 for more in-depth information.)

1. **A is for Accept:** Accept that Spiritual Communication is real, and you are fully capable of communicating spiritually.
2. **C is for Claim:** Claim Spiritual Communication for yourself and start opening yourself to it and using it.
3. **U is for Utilize:** Utilize one or more of the many tools and strategies to activate, expand, and strengthen your Intuitive Abilities and Spiritual Connection such as:
   a. Praying: Asking Your Source/God for help and staying aware of the messages that come
   b. Meditating
   c. Appreciating
   d. Using a pendulum
   e. Muscle testing
   f. Walking a labyrinth or using a finger labyrinth
   g. Divine Journaling
   h. Decoding your Dreams
   i. Decoding your Messages
   j. Creating an Individual Intuition Lexicon of your symbols, signs, and their meanings
4. **T is for Trust:** Trust your feelings, messages, and the signs that you are receiving.
5. **E is for Enjoy:** Enjoy the process and journey of Spiritual Communication.

References

Anthony, Mark. 2021. *The Afterlife Frequency*. California: New World Library.

Aron, Elaine N. 1996. *The Highly Sensitive Person: How to Thrive When the World Overwhelms You*. New York: Broadway Books.

Caputo, Theresa, star. 2011-2019. *Long Island Medium*. Magilla Entertainment. Aired on TLC network.

Caputo, Teresa, star. 2011. *Long Island Medium*. Season 1, Episode 7, "Blessing & a Curse." Produced by Brian Flanagan. Magilla Entertainment, October 23. Aired on TLC network.

Carradine, David, star. 1973. *Kung Fu*. Season 1, Episode 12, "Superstition." Directed by Charles S. Dubin, April 5. Aired on ABC network.

Hay, Louise. 1984. *You Can Heal Your Life*. California: Hay House. Reprints 1984, 1987, 1999.

Walsch, Neale Donald. 1995. *Conversations with God: Book 1*. Newburyport, MA: Hampton Roads Publishing Company. Reprint New York: G.P. Putnam's Sons, 1996.

About the Author

Karoleen Fober is a spiritual teacher, author, Intuitive Business and Life Mastery Coach and Mentor, and a Divine Energy Reader. Since 2001, when she created All Inspired Coaching and Consulting, Karoleen has provided numerous workshops and thousands of personal consultations to clients all over the United States.

Karoleen works with Heart-centered Entrepreneurs, Transformational Leaders, Light Workers, and people on their spiritual journeys.

She teaches God's Divine Universal Laws and Manifesting principles, along with simple ways to expand, develop, and master your intuitive gifts to communicate spiritually and receive Divine messages, so you can navigate your energetic well-being, business and career, relationships, and spiritual growth—quickly and easily, with confidence.

Karoleen has a BS in Early Childhood Education from Iowa State University, is a former preschool handicapped teacher, and owned her own financial planning business for fifteen years.

When not writing, coaching, or doing Divine readings, Karoleen enjoys keeping up with her family and eight grandchildren, growing dahlias, tending her gardens, and reading. She and her husband Gary split their time between Cedar Falls, Iowa, and Southwest Florida. Connect with Karoleen at KaroleenFober.com.

www.ingramcontent.com/pod-product-compliance
Lightning Source LLC
Chambersburg PA
CBHW070906120626
46546CB00001B/156